GODCIDENCE: Cl
BY CHRIST

GHT

Printed in the United States of America

First Printing, 2017

10 9 8 7 6 5 4 3 2 1

ISBN 978-1974134502

ACKNOWLEDGMENT

I would like to give my thanks to Travis Gerlecz for the cover illustration and to Aidan Barrett-Wokurka for the inside artwork.

I would like to give special thanks to my family for always loving me and encouraging me to be a better version of myself today then I was the day before. I love you, Mom XOXO

Amy Zimaniak,

Thank you so much
for donating you time
to my teen Parents
Ernisha & Steven. You
really made them feel
comfortable & welcomed.
They both have their guard
up and you were able to
break through it with
your abundnet kindness.
   I pray my story encourages
you. Please Share it with
someone you Love.
God Bless
Danny Baiden

FOREWORD

"Godcidence: Chased by the Devil but Caught by Christ" is an emotionally heart-wrenching book that shows the brutality of life and the everlasting beauty of our Savior.

Read it. Cry. Be moved.

When you finish the last words be ready to share this story with others - anyone wondering if God is real needs to read this book today!

David M Yajko, *Development Director, ICCM Life Center*

INTRODUCTION

My life has been insane from the beginning. My father was a loan shark for many years in South Omaha, and he never left the house without a gun. I have seen, and been subject to, a few horrible crimes in my life. Shoot-outs, drugs, and primal fear were regular occurrences in my childhood home. I can tell you what it feels like to not know love and be filled with hate for the whole world and everyone in it; to not care who you hurt or if you even wake up tomorrow.

I remember how much I hated this so-called God for what was happening to my sister, mother and me through all those years. I grew up to be a proud, self-proclaimed atheist and I hated any talk of God because I knew there wasn't one. My perspective was that man had created God, the Easter Bunny and Santa Claus as a bunch of crap to feed to us as children so we would grow up to carry a guilty conscience whenever we behaved badly. Men who wanted the next generation to behave kindly, and not just murder and rob other people, had created these stories of consequences for your actions to spoon-feed generations.

I understand the stories in this book may sound crazy to you, but I'd like to give you an inside look at the mind of a mentally and physically abused child who stumbles on God and by His grace gets saved and then wonderfully used for His glory. This is my testimony and collection of the signs and wonders I have been privileged to be a part of.

I understand what I went through is extreme, but God had a plan for me the whole time. My perspective of this world has changed dramatically and continues to develop every day. I can see where once I was blind; I am now filled with a joy and peace that surpasses all understanding. I want to show you how God has transformed my heart and freed my mind, and how to walk in that peace confidently with Christ.

I woke up today with a burden to write down all that God has done for me, all the wonders and signs He has let me see and be part of. There are so many of them that they have become a normal part of my life, perhaps too normal! Unfortunately, I loathe writing; you might as well ask me to diet and exercise every day during the holiday season! Yet the burden is real and heavy on my heart. So, here we go ...

(Before we begin, I should probably warn you that you'll encounter lots of very crude language and some fairly graphic descriptions in this book, which is necessary to convey just what life was really like for me and my family!)

Danny

CHAPTER 1: THIEVING AND THIRD DATES

My mother, Christine Dahir, grew up in South Omaha, Nebraska off of 11th and Dorcas. During the 1970's, downtown Omaha was called Hippie Town by some because of the flower-child hippies that could be seen hanging out all over. Omaha was a small city and was well-known for its many cattle stockyards. Christine's father, George Dahir, appreciated hard work was the owner of a gas station and car dealership on 13th and Deer Park. The business did well, as it sat right next to Rosenblatt Stadium, famous for the College World Series. He loved to race different kinds of cars and had many trophies that still hang from the walls of his huge, red-bricked four-car garage.

Looking back, they would have been one of the coolest and financially well-off families in the working middle class section of South Omaha, or 'South O', as we called it. My mother was born at St. Joseph's hospital on March 5, 1955. She was one of seven children. At the age of four, her baby brother Michael had chased a ball out into the street; he ran between the parked cars unseen by the driver coming down the road and was hit hard. Christine, was only six at the time, was seated on the front porch of their home when she heard the tires screech. Her older sister, Denise, held her tightly and rocked her while they cried together on the porch. Michael, nicknamed Willy, suffered severe brain damage and was declared mentally retarded.

When Willy was younger, he was very strong and sometimes violent. He would spit in Christine's hair and punch out windows in the house all the time. One time, he replaced all the salad dressing with his urine and didn't tell anyone. Later, everyone at the dinner table kept sniffing the vinaigrette-filled air. Willy was excited to inform them that he had been using the vinaigrette as cologne, so he had filled the bottles back up with pee. He is a silly old man now who loves to hug and tell jokes.

Jamie, their youngest daughter, takes care of him in the same small red brick home they grew up in.

Jamie, Christine's sister, is ten years younger than Christine. Now I hate to boast, but my aunt Jamie is the most beautiful women I ever laid eyes on. Her hair was the perfect brunette 'Farrah Fawcett cut' of the 1980's. Their brothers, George Jr., and David both played in rock bands and both still perform today. Christine was in eleventh grade at South High when she met my father.

It is important for you to understand where she was mentally so you can grasp why she stayed with him for thirty-three years. Christine seemed to be spoiled by her Mom and Dad. She would cruise around in a brand-new 1972 baby blue Mustang convertible that her daddy had bought her for her 17th birthday. She would hang out at the McDonald's after school and play spin the bottle with the boys in the back alley. She recalls only doing this once, just to try and kiss a boy named Jimmy. I read a report card signed by her mother that read: "If my daughter Krissy is getting bad grades in your classroom, then it is a result of your teaching ability and not the efforts of my daughter." Krissy was a spoiled seventeen-year-old with no real rules and with no one who was raising her to be an adult. She was just learning on her own as she walked through life.

Christine said her mother, Donna, loved to play Bingo at South Sokol and could be found there any weekend night. She was a grumpy woman and always seemed to be mad at her husband, George. He had cheated on her with her best friend and was caught red-handed under the south Omaha Bridge. She never forgave him, and when they would argue he would remind her of what he had done by whistling "Hey Jude" by the Beatles. The adulteress' name was Jude, of course.

My Father, Danny Gardner, was born in Bellevue, Nebraska on May 5, 1949 to Jack and Winona. Danny was the fourth child born of ten brothers and sisters. He was always a very naughty little boy. At the age of five, he snuck upstairs and peed through the floor vent onto his aunt's head, who was seated at the kitchen table with his own mother. They grew up very poor, so poor they would get one pair of shoes for the year; when those shoes were done, they were done wearing shoes. Danny and his brothers would be so hungry that in the middle of the night they would crawl up the basement stairs on their bellies to attempt to steal a can of beans from the cabinet, only to get caught due to squeaky stairs and yelled at by their dad, Jack.

Jack would steal salt and pepper shakers from places and had a cabinet full of them Danny learned how to be a thief, stealing from everyone (including his mother). Danny was still living with his parents when he was sent to the Kearney Home for Boys for stealing furniture from a neighbor's home. Danny always suspected his mom had got mad at him and turned him into the police because she was the one who suggested he steal the neighbor's furniture. Danny also learned how to be abusive, He told me that his father came home drunk one night and started a fight with Winona. He was so enraged that he made Winona strip her clothes off and stand outside naked in snow. He made it to ninth grade before he dropped out of High School. He told the story of how he tripped a teacher in school who was making his way down the hall. The teacher walked with a cane – after he tripped the teacher Danny took the cane.

Later, Danny and his dad would go out to the bars, Jack's mouth would pick a fight that Danny's fists would always finish. One time, Jack picked a fight with a woman at the bar and Danny walked right up to her and knocked her out right on the stool at the bar where she sat. He was always trying to prove how ruthless he was to his father and to his four brothers. Dan would secretly carry a roll of quarters balled up under his grip to assist him when he knocked people out. He loved to fight and for many years he was in a bar every weekend getting drunk to get into a fight. He told me back then there were only three things to do in life and they were to get drunk, get into a fight and sleep with girls. He said he slept with a different girl every weekend.

Back in 1972, Krissy was a beautiful sophomore attending South High School over on 24th St. One day, Krissy befriended a girl named Pamela and she volunteered to give Pamela a ride to her home after school. Pamela was gorgeous like her sisters, a lot of fun to talk to and would tell wild tales, like the time she survived a barracuda attack out in the ocean, but that her friend had died during the attack. They pulled up to a tiny white house in the ghetto and Pamela invited Krissy to come in.

Inside, seated at the kitchen table playing with the deck of cards in his hands, was Danny. Danny had a few homemade tattoos by this time popping off his muscular body and was now twenty-three years old. Krissy was still just seventeen. Danny talked his sister Pamela and Krissy into hanging out with him and playing cards. Ten minutes later he convinced Krissy into playing strip poker. As Danny was winning, Krissy was not taking her clothes off. Later, Danny lost and wouldn't take his pants off so Krissy said, "You owe me." Pamela said, "Make him kiss you. He owes you a kiss." With very little persuasion they scooted their chairs towards each other and passionately kissed.

She said he was the best kisser in the whole world and by that time she had done plenty of kissing. Danny was very sexy and even looked like Tony Danza from "Who's the Boss?". She would always be compared to Cher in the 1980's. Together they were the couple in the movie Grease, Danny and Sandy. They always tried to look and dress cooler than everyone else. Everyone seemed to whisper about them, even when I was growing up as their child. Everyone that would meet them just thought they were the coolest.

Krissy immediately heard the story of Danny getting his heart broken recently by a girl named Frenchie. After Frenchie ended their relationship, Danny was so upset he broke into her house and destroyed everything. He even killed her pet bird, but Krissy just brushed it off as nothing much for her to worry about.

On their first date he tried to impress her by punching out car side windows. He pulled his car up behind a parked car and got out of the driver's seat. He told Krissy, "Watch this" and then walked up to the driver's side door of the parked car and punched it as hard as he could. Krissy said the window didn't break. All she kept thinking was how crazy he was, and later they parked in an alley and made out in Danny's car all evening. He tried to put his hand down her shirt and she wouldn't let him. The next night on their second date, there was more parking in back alleys and making out but Krissy really liked him so she said she wanted to make him wait for it.

Finally, on the third date Danny couldn't hold out any longer and just proposed and she said yes, so they drove to Rock Port, Missouri. By the time they arrived in Rock Port it was the next morning and also Sunday, so everything was closed. This meant they would have to wait to be married. Krissy decided she should call home to let her worried parents in on her adventures. Her mother answered immediately only to hear her daughter say, "Mom, I am in Rockport Missouri with Danny and we are getting married." Donna's heart must have sunk as she handed the phone to George, Krissy's dad. He talked to her and convinced them to come back home to Omaha and have a wedding the traditional way. They agreed, so Danny and Krissy moved in with Krissy's parents while they worked out the details and planned for the wedding.

Dan and Krissy's father never intended to get along with each other. I believe George and Donna put their best foot forward to stand by their daughter's decision to marry Danny. Donna even let them sleep in the same bedroom together as long as, "Danny keeps his shorts on". So George and Donna were a bit naive. They had been having sex since the third date.

CHAPTER 2: HONEYMOONS AND HOGTIES

George decided to peek into Dan's past and see who this man was that was stealing his daughter. George found out Danny had spent time in a boy's home for troubled youth. Donna came to Krissy with this information one evening, only to find Krissy was offended and it put a wedge between her and her parents. In a rage, Chris and Dan moved out and in with Maggie and Steve, who lived in a tiny home close to Christine's parents. Maggie and Christine had grown up together and were best friends and cousins.

The plans were being put in place, invitations sent out and the wedding hall was booked. Dan and Chris regularly got drunk and played cards while living with Maggie and Steve. Dan would talk bad about all of Christine's family and how stupid they were, all day every day. He would shine a light on their flaws and twist words to make them sound like terrible people. He was also a very funny guy and everybody enjoyed his crazy ways and conversation.

One evening as the four were driving around town, Dan and Steve were riding up front with Chris and Maggie giggling in the back, Maggie brought up the subject of marriage. Dan said playfully, "Hell, I'd marry that bitch in the back seat right now." Christine smiled and replied flirtatiously, "Bet". This was the moment in time that solidified my fate. The four kids drove to the courthouse and Dan and Chris were married. On the way, Krissy couldn't help but sing the old classic, "Going to the chapel and we're going to get married". She stood there in front of the judge in her tank top and wearing cut-off shorts and Dan was wearing blue jeans with flip flops.

With Maggie and Steve as their witnesses, they were married. During the judge's marriage ceremony, Dan accidentally burned Christine in the leg with his cigarette. Christine felt like a woman and couldn't care less about what her parents thought. She was head over heels in love with the wild boy from the bad side of town. Dan would always say through the years, that he married her because she had the biggest titties he had ever seen.

They spent their honeymoon night at the old Flamingo hotel down on highway 75; it was a tiny, dirty little hotel right by Fontenelle Forest. Every time we drove past it Mom would tell us the story of their marriage and honeymoon, and I just always wished they had never even met. Dan spent the whole honeymoon night at the bar, playing pool with Steve. When he finally made his way to the room, he brought a bottle of champagne with him that the manager of the hotel had given him in honor of their marriage.

I asked my mom a few times when was the first time she saw a red flag with Dad. She told me they were sleeping at Maggie and Steve's house one night and Dan had gotten really drunk. She had passed out on the sofa and woke up to the noise she heard coming from the floor. Dan was sitting up against the wall and had a pocket knife out with a four-inch blade on it. She was scared to get up or even speak; it was so dark in the room and so she just watched. She saw Dan mumbling and yelling at himself saying, "Fine! You just want me to die then," as he was hitting himself in the face. "Fine! I'll just fucking kill myself then." He took the knife and stabbed himself right in his belly. She saw the stab wound and never really gave it much thought. Maybe she felt sorry for him, who knows.

When I asked her when was the first time that Dan hit her, she told me the four of them, Chris, Dan, Maggie and Steve, were staying in some tiny cabins just past the South Omaha Bridge, down the road from a strip club (the type of cabins for people hiding from the law). Dan had gotten drunk and spent the whole night tearing the place apart, screaming and yelling. When the sun finally came up, he was still at it with no one getting any sleep.

They all got into their cars and took off with Maggie and Steve following close behind. Dan was talking crazy nonsense and he also had his knife out. He looked at Chris seated next to him and spontaneously punched her in the face, breaking her eye glasses. When he punched her the car swerved and his knife fell down on the floor board. He reached down to get it and his car swerved again, driving off into a ditch over by Lake Manawa. The cops came and Dan fed them a story, doing his best song and dance routine to make the cops laugh and want to be cool with him. They bought it and their car was towed out of the ditch. The cops just assumed Chris's glasses broke from the impact.

Most women would never have made it to this point with Dan. They would have run for the hills the very first sign of crazy. But Chris was naive and carried a heart of gold. She loved him and was sure it would all work out with time and love. He was the sexiest, toughest man she had ever seen. In my mother's defense, when Dan walked down the street the crowds of people would part for him. He had a presence about him like a famous actor; people would notice him and women would swoon over him. He had a way with people; when he started to speak, people would circle to listen. He was called the king of one-liners by many.

His words would flow like an improv comedian who looked and dressed like someone of importance with a street edge. He was mistaken for famous TV actors a few times, even while I was around him. I recall women following him and thinking he was Charles Bronson. Even as a child, when I walked through a store with my dad it felt like I was cool or I was tough. Just walking next to him made you respected by all the people around you and my words just can't explain that. I am forty years old and have met a million different people in my life, yet I have never met anyone who had the same presence and light that shone from my dad. Even though it was a harmful light, it still shone and people had to take notice.

Still living with Maggie and Steve, Dan had gotten mad at Chris while they were playing cards and decided to teach Chris a lesson for something and tied her up. He pinned her to the ground and took rope to tie her hands and legs up. Like a cattle rancher would do to a calf, he tied her hands together behind her back and tied both of her feet to her hands. Cattle ranchers call it hog tied. He positioned her on her side lying on the floor next to his feet at the card table.

I can't imagine how uncomfortable and scary it must have been for little seventeen-year-old Chris. Dan then took a pillowcase and put it over her head, while he still continued to play cards. Maggie and Steve would have been too scared to do anything, in case it directed his anger onto them. Dan took his beer in his hand and throughout the night would pour it over Chris's face. This would suffocate her each time for a few seconds, like the infamous waterboarding. She remembers thinking she was going to die and she remembers Dan laughing the whole time like it was funny as she wiggled and cried out loud.

Through the first year, Chris would try and do little things to stand up to Dan. One time he had really upset her, so she wrote "Fuck you" on his favorite black Stetson cowboy hat. But every time she would stand up for herself he would beat her down ten times harder. He slowly and methodically removed all her family and friends from her life. One by one, he convinced her they were out to sabotage the true love they had for each other. It was going to be the two of them together forever, best friends. She was his partner for life and now she was pregnant at eighteen with their first child together.

CHAPTER 3: PREGNANCIES AND PEPI

Christine's first child was never born into this world. Dan had punched her in the stomach early into the pregnancy and she miscarried. Still only seventeen, she became pregnant again; this time the baby made it through the pregnancy and my older sister Charity was born on March 12, 1974. Dan and Christine were living in a tiny home on 9th Street in South Omaha. Dan was working at the slaughterhouse, lugging beef all day long. It is a rough job of hard labor, but it was all he could get without being able to read.

Christine had a tiny black poodle named Pepi that she loved very much and treated like her own child. When they brought Charity home from the hospital, Dan walked into the front door and placed Charity, two days old, down on the floor in her car seat. Pepi ran right up to the baby, sniffed her up and down then raised his little leg and peed in her face. Dan pulled out the large eight-inch buck knife he carried on his belt and chased the dog under the couch. He was trying to stab Pepi in the head, but couldn't reach the dog. After trying for a few seconds and moving the couch around, the dog was too fast and Dan gave up. He told Chris, "You have exactly one fucking minute to get rid of that dog or I'm cutting its fucking head off. And if I ever see that dog again I'm cutting its head off. Do you understand me, bitch?" Christine nodded her head in agreement and as soon as Dan left the room she grabbed her dog up and left the house. Christine gave Pepi to the young girl who loved Pepi and lived just down the street.

They both thought Charity was an ugly baby at first, because she was completely bald with a huge cone-shaped head. Her cone went down in a few days and she grew beautiful brunette hair in its place. Dan and Christine loved baby Charity unconditionally. Dan played with her often and she was a little precious princess in his eyes. Dan would always do his best to protect her from all men and any harm from others.

A few weeks later, Dan had all his boys over who worked with him at the slaughterhouse. Now this was a rough and tough crowd of guys and Dan was their ringleader. They were all hanging out drinking on the front lawn one fine sunny afternoon and had all heard the story of Pepi the poodle. As the boys sat around laughing at all Dan's stories, one guy looked up and noticed a black poodle prancing down the street. He said, "Hey Danny, ain't that the dog you said if you ever saw it again you were gonna cut its head off?" They all laughed and started calling for the dog to come over. The men lined the fence and clapped their hands chanting, "Here Pepi, here boy."

Little Pepi ran over to them excitedly. Pepi was picked up and tossed to Dan so he pulled out that eight-inch buck knife from its holster. In a few cuts, the dog's head was off and he tossed it over to everyone's feet. This caused all the men to roar in laughter. Christine was inside standing in the kitchen with Dan's beautiful sister Tamera when they heard the commotion coming from outside. Tamera watched in horror as Danny cut off Christine's poodle's head. Chris looked at Tamera and knew what had happened without even having to ask but she did anyway. She asked Tamera, "He cut Pepi's head off, didn't he?" knowing the answer would be yes. Christine snatched Charity up in her arms and left Dan for the first time since they had been together. She went back home to live with her mom and dad. Dan called the house relentlessly and even sent over several bouquets of flowers. He begged and pleaded and made promises to Christine he would never keep. He would show up and plead with her father for mercy until finally she would give in and go back to Dan. This happened several times before I was even born and every so often during my childhood.

Christine got pregnant immediately after Charity and miscarried when she fell that winter and slipped on the ice. Then she miscarried again when she had a few drinks and fell down a set of stairs. She said she simply bounced on her butt down them, and the baby was gone. Now she was nineteen years old and pregnant with me, Dan was now twenty-five. They lived in a small white home with black trim at 1437 South 18th Street when I was born. Dan had started smoking pot, which calmed him down quite a bit. He was slightly better at controlling his anger, but the alcohol made him mad. So when my mom went into labor with me she was in pain and Dan asked the doctor if it would be alright if she smoked a little weed to calm her down. The doctor gave him the thumbs up and left the room.

Back then there was no ultrasound machine and family would tell you if you were going to have a boy or a girl based off of how high your belly sat or what things you craved to eat while you were pregnant. So according to the old wives' tale, her belly sat high and she was going to have a boy. It was a surprise to her to have given birth to a girl, so she had no name chosen for me. Days went by and a nurse had suggested going ahead and naming the baby Danny anyway, and so she did. I was born on September 18, 1976 and named a few days later Danny Marie Gardner after my father. But I would always be known as Dan Jr., Little Dan or Baby Dan.

Christine would go on to have two more pregnancies, one miscarriage, and one abortion, and then started birth control; they had decided two children was enough. My sister and I were over two years apart and unfortunately it seemed that they had already spent their love on Charity and didn't have much left for me. Mom says you spend money on cameras and stuff for the first one, but by the time the second one comes around you don't have time for all that. So I don't have any pictures of me when I was a baby. We have one picture though and we think it's me, does that count? Charity was always very smart and pretty. She was the one Dad would regularly call the twinkle in his eye. He would play-fully pat me on the head and introduce me as his "Spacey little fuck-up" named Danny Jr., just like her dad. Yes, it hurt, and they were not al-ways playful pats - sometimes he would hit me so hard it would make me stumble forward as he said it.

I can remember some good times when my dad would love on us after he would come home from work. And I must say our family's Christ-mases were simply the best. We would always go to see Santa and Dad would take us out to see the Christmas lights every Christmas eve. The four of us would climb into the car and head out to drive around town looking at all the Christmas lights; when we would return, the presents had appeared magically under the tree. Christmas went down in his-tory as our only flawless, no fighting, and no drama holiday. It was al-ways spent together around a tree in love and laughter. Once we re-turned from our Christmas Eve cruise to find footprints of reindeer in the snow and when we went inside there were no presents under the tree.

We were so sad until Dad noticed something strange hiding inside the tree. We looked up and Dad picked up Charity to lift her up and pull out a note straight from Santa. It read, "Dear Charity and Danny, I did not have time to put your presents under the tree this year be-cause you came home so fast and surprised me. So I had to run out the back door after you came inside to put the presents out on the front porch. Signed, Merry Christmas, Love, Santa." Now our little minds were blown away because we had just come in through the front door and there were no presents. We rushed to the door and to our wonder-ful surprise Santa was real and the presents were there just like he had promised. Dad was so slick; he had snuck out the back door while we sat in disbelief that Santa had not come this year and placed a sky-high pile of presents on the front porch. Unfortunately, that was the best part of those eight hard years growing up in the house on 18th Street.

When I was five years old, I had gotten into my mother's purse and found a piece of chocolate and ate it. She came out of the kitchen to find me sitting under the kitchen table high on mescaline saying, "Look at all the bugs, Mommy", as I tried to catch invisible bugs around me. She realized I had been in her purse and had eaten their drugs. Mescaline is a psychedelic alkaloid known for its hallucinogenic effects, similar to LSD. She took me to the hospital and the doctor apparently told both my parents that it was too late to pump my stomach and to just sit with me and let me ride the trip out. After the doctor left the room, a nurse came in and advised my parents that the doctor was going to call the cops and they had better get out of there. So they snatched me up and fled from the hospital to avoid any charges. My father would later tell everyone this story through the years and people would laugh at how funny it was.

Dad was drinking a lot and we would get spanked all the time for any reason. I especially would get spanked for everything, like sitting on the couch because I was not allowed on it, we would have to sit on the floor. I would also find myself getting beat for crying for getting beat or just not getting something for Dad fast enough. My hair was very long and all one length; I would tuck my long bangs behind my ears and Dad would catch me and yell at me, then beat me with a belt.

We spent our summers only outside and swimming in the horse tank in the back yard. One summer, Dad bought us a baby chicken and a duck to play with. He built a cage for them and it was really fun having a baby duck to swim with in the horse tank. We came home from school and found a giant white husky eating them both ravenously. We ran in the house screaming for Dad. Dad jumped up out of bed into action, grabbed a 45-caliber pistol and ran out of the house in his white BVD underwear and shot that dog. It always blew his mind that that dog ran away after being shot with a 45 caliber. Dad was always our hero, making him the coolest dad ever.

If I didn't like someone, I knew my dad would beat him half to death. Everyone who came into our house through the years would fearfully treat my sister and me with kindness and dollar bills. The house on 18th Street sat on top of a steep hill. To get home you would have to go up about thirty steps to the front door. To the left was an empty lot owned by the "Old Man" whose house sat way back on the street behind our house. On the right side was a large family I only met a few times, probably because my dad decided to shoot their dog one night when he was drunk. He killed that German Shepherd, he said, because "They didn't pick up their dog shit and that was why we had rats in our house". He would tease us with the rats, a few times, putting them in the bathroom sink and toilet to scare us.

Dad even pinned a rat down with a knife by its tail. Then he took another knife and teased the rat, forcing it to bite down on the knife. It was so scary, yet somehow it was really cool to me how crazy my dad was. When we were around five and seven years old, Dad would have my sister Charity and I sit out on our front porch and make oinking pig sounds to our neighbor lady when she would come home from work. We would sneak out there with Dad's instigation and wait for her to get out of her car. She was a round woman and as children it made sense to us. Dad watched gleefully through the blinds as we taunted the lady and then ran inside so we could all laugh at her.

These were good childhood times to us. The old man who lived next door was about seventy years old and had a beautiful garden that ran all the way around his old white house. Charity and I would sneak up the hill to steal his flowers for our mom. He would get so mad at us that one time he chased me all the way down the hill with a sickle in his hand. I was scared to death and ran inside our house and told my dad. Dad came out and threatened to kill him, then made fun of him for being so old and all alone up there in that house. He told that old man the only reason he was such a dick was because he ain't had any pussy besides his dead mother's. Then Dad called my mom over and pulled her tits out and jiggled them saying, "Here you go old man, something for you to jerk yourself off to later." Then he spit the biggest cigarette stained yellow loogie into the old man's face. It looked like an egg yolk as it ran down his cheek and brushed passed his lips. The cops were called by the old man and Dad told them, "I was just talking and you know how you get when you're excited sometimes and spit just flies out". I knew that old man was lucky that day that my dad didn't just kill him.

Back then things seemed so exciting with the cops over nearly every other weekend. Dad would have guys over the house from work and they would hang out, get drunk, make bets, and fight. Dad would shoot out the street lights when times seemed too dull. I would walk around the house collecting beer bottle caps and listen in on all the fun conversations. It was always fun times when people where over because Dad would be putting on "The Dan Show", and we all would watch and cheer.

CHAPTER 4: BIRDS AND BOA CONSTRICTORS

I grew to love animals more than any little kid could. I spent a lot of time alone with frogs, turtles, kittens and snakes. Dad and his buddies were all outside one fine spring day when I found my very first nest of baby birds. I took the nest out of the tree and marched proudly to show my father my discovery. He was standing in the front yard talking to his friends when he turned around to see why I had tugged on his pant leg. I said, "Look Dad, it's a nest of baby birds." He said, "Those ain't baby birds, Danny. Those are grenades!" He reached into the nest still in my hands and grabbed a baby bird. He yelled, "Fire in the hole," and bit the head off the baby bird, spat it out into the air, and then threw the body across the yard. I started crying and took off running, while Dad and his friends roared in laughter.

My sister and I would spend our days tag-teamed to catch garter snakes. She would step on the head and I would pick it up by the tail, and sometimes we would take them to Dad to whip in the air like a wet towel and split their heads in two. I can remember catching tons of garter snakes and putting them in a jar to watch them bake in the sun. I remember putting a baby garter snake in my mouth to freak out my sister. We wouldn't be allowed inside the house sometimes for a long period of time. We would play outside all day long and only get to drink from the garden hose. Sometimes, we would be hungry and my sister would talk me into stepping on a bee so we could have an excuse to ring the doorbell and maybe get to come inside.

Living on 18th Street, I had gotten very attached to a feral cat. I called it Whitefish in the winter and Snowflake in the summer. I was there the day she was born and months later when her mom abandoned her on a rainy night. So when Whitefish had a litter of five kittens, I was so excited. I loved spending my days playing with them outside. Dad yelled out from the front door one day and told me to round up my kittens and put them in a brown paper sack he handed me. So I did, because I always did exactly what my father said the second he asked me to, out of fear of getting beat. I brought him the kittens and we loaded up in the car.

Charity and I sat in the back seat as Dad drove down the road away from our house. He got to a busy street and stopped the car right in the street. He stapled the paper bag shut - then opened the driver's side door of the car. He set the bag down in the center of the street, looked back at me and then drove off. I watched in horror as cars drove by the bag until we turned the corner. I don't remember him saying anything to me. He would do crazy things and watch us to see our reactions. I think he did things sometimes to just keep us in fear and so we would remember he was a monster.

We had a pet bird we named Tweety, who hung in his small cage in our dining room - just a regular old cheap parakeet you would buy from the pet store. Well, Mom accidentally fed it the wrong type of food so it died over the winter. I took Tweety out and buried him in the snow in the lot next to our house. I would regularly dig Tweety up to take him snow sledding down the old man's hill with me. I decided it would be cool to see what he would look like with his head cut off so I carried his frozen body in the house and asked Dad to cut his head off.

He obliged me and cut Tweety's head off for me right at the kitchen table. I walked back outside with the body in my right hand and the head in my left. I can remember hitting a bump while sledding down the hill and Tweety's head bouncing off to the left while the body flew through the air on the right. I was becoming a weird kid.

Dad worked at Northern States Beef slaughterhouse off of 42nd and L St. Once in a while he would bring me home a fetus sealed up in an alcohol-filled jar. I would keep it for weeks kind of like a pet and thought it was the coolest thing ever. I took one to school in Kindergarten for show and tell. I didn't understand why all the other kids didn't love looking at it as much as I did. My teacher was not very pleased. Unfortunately, the paper bag I was carrying the jar in had clipped the cement stairs on my way into Castelar School. The jar began to leak alcohol all through the hallway and finish seeping down my teacher's desk. The teacher made my mom come up to school and clean it all up.

It was absolutely the best fun to go pick Dad up from work at the slaughterhouse. He worked on the kill floor and he would come outside sometimes and spit a cow eyeball onto the windshield of our car and we would all scream and laugh. He even wrapped a cow eyeball up in plastic for me with a rope chain so I could wear one around my neck. I went to the grocery store and pointed it at everyone I saw and told them, "I got my eye on you." I loved it and thought Dad was so cool for giving it to me. He would take Charity and I out onto the kill floor and parade us around. I would feel so special. Blood covered every inch of the floor and the walls.

A slaughterhouse is a loud cement catacomb; a maze of men and machinery with cows and pieces of cows hanging from the ceiling. It was the coolest thing I had ever seen as a kid. Dad would march me right through the place and everyone was always covered in blood and happy to see me. They would run over to pat me on the head or shake my hand because I was "Dan Gardner's daughter". He even took me where the cows come into the building alive and a gun comes down from the ceiling and shoots a bolt into the brain of the cow. The boy running the gun was my dad's friend, and to gross us out he stuck his finger in the hole he created and licked the brains off his finger. We laughed together and to me it was all just great.

All the guys at the packing house looked like they loved him. They would run out to shake Mom's hand and would call her Mrs. G. You see, my dad was a loan shark. This meant if a guy borrowed fifty dollars from my dad on Tuesday, come Friday that guy owed him a hundred dollars. Dad had a black book full of people who owed him money. Sometimes they owed him for losing at craps against him or making a bet on random stuff. We would show up to pick Dad up from work and Dad would get into the driver seat and we would ride along when he went to collect.

One time, Charity and I were in the back seat when Dad tailed a guy back to his home. Dad didn't explain anything to us on the way to the guy's house. We parked and watched the guy walk into the house. Dad got out and walked onto the front patio to knock on the inner door. A lady came to the door and Dad pointed down at the ground. He bent down to pick up something and it was a tiny puppy. They had a litter of puppies on the front porch and Charity and I got so excited. We knew now that Dad was surprising us with a puppy. I can remember getting so excited. Then Dad pulled out his buck knife and cut the puppy's head off. He wiped his blade on the head, threw the head to the ground and walked back to the car. We sat in the back seat and cried. The guy came out behind him with the money owed to my father.

Even though we lived in the ghetto, Dad made and spent a lot of money on hot guns and gold for himself. He also had a nice Harley Davidson that he kept parked next to the house. Our walls were all covered in guns. There were hundreds of them, ranging from fully automatics to classic revolvers engraved with gold inlay. I know because we had to hide them a few times throughout our childhood. Dad also had thieves who worked for him. The two main thieves were called Rick and Mark, both about seventeen years old. He had met them walking down our street one day, slashing everyone's tires for fun. Dad said, "Listen, you little cock suckers. If you slash my fucking tires, I'll fucking kill you!" One of the boys said, "Fuck you, old man. You can't do shit to us without going to jail. We're under eighteen." Dad knew they were right and invited them up. He made a business proposition with those two boys and they were best of friend/enemies for years. I remember having a huge a crush on Mark and my sister had a crush on Rick.

They would steal anything my dad requested - guns, gold, bikes; once they even stole the chalice from the Catholic Church by our house. Dad had always thought the chalices were made of real gold, but once he got his hands on one he realized they weren't.

He felt a little bad for stealing it now that it wasn't gold and had the boys take it back. Those boys were cunning. They would crawl into your house through your bedroom windows and slide on their bellies and steal your gun next to you in your nightstand as you slept. One of them went to help an old lady start her lawnmower; he told her to go get the gas in the garage and took off down the street with her mower. Other people caught wind of Dad and would show up with everything you can possibly imagine; my dad would almost always buy it and sell it for profit.

Here are some things that showed up at our door: an alligator in two coolers that were cut and glued together; a 6-foot boa constrictor that Dad was going to keep, but after we fed it once and it pooped, he decided it stunk so bad that he sold it; a bucket of gold rings, watches and necklaces; even a truck full of BIC lighters. But my favorite story to tell is the bird from Henry Doorly Zoo. Not just any bird, there was a mascot parrot back then. It was a macaw, the big one. I guess it sat in its own cage at the old entrance to the Zoo.

Now it was the middle of winter and there was a strange knock at the door; like usual, it meant something exciting. Dad let the guys in and they had a large metal trash can with them. They removed the lid and out popped this giant bird that was blind in one eye. Dad said, "What the fuck am I supposed to do with this?" After some back and forth bickering and bartering, Dad bought the bird for $20. He told the boys to go home and then he called the cops.

Two officers came to our front door and Dad kept them right there. Dad said, "Look, some kids came to my house and said they found this bird, so I told them I'll give you fifty bucks for it because I noticed it had a Henry Doorly zoo bracelet wrapped around its leg. I knew if they let this thing go it would freeze to death out there. All I want is to turn it in and get my fifty bucks back." So the cops, according to my mother, called some bigwig at the zoo. This guy was pissed off about the bird being stolen and wanted my dad arrested for buying stolen property and/or stealing his bird. One officer agreed with that guy's opinion, and the other agreed with my dad's. Well, needless to say, we ended up with a one-year membership to the zoo, which we figured was equivalent to the fifty bucks. Dad was always pissed he didn't get the fifty dollars and we were just happy we got to go to the zoo that year.

CHAPTER 5: SNOWBLOWERS AND CIGARETTES

One winter, my dad had asked the boys to get him all the snow blowers they could find; weeks later, after the snow came, Dad forgot he had even asked for them. We woke up one morning to find Dad in a panic running from window to window. Peeking through the blinds you saw tire tracks in fresh snow leading up to our house. He started grabbing all the guns off the walls and tossing them to us saying, "Hide the guns, girls. Hide them under your mattresses." "Fuck Christine, I'm going to jail!" There were so many guns under our mattresses; it was obvious to anyone who looked at the beds. It looked like bodies were hidden under there. It sat so high the sides of the top mattress didn't even touch the bottom mattress anymore. The doorbell rang and Mom answered. It was just Dad's thieves. They had gone all around the neighborhood stealing everyone's snow blowers and took them through the fresh snow right up to our house. We spent that morning making hundreds of snow angels with adult men all over the streets and yard. Dad was so pissed at them for being clumsy; I don't think he even paid them anything for the snow blowers. But Dad was able to sell them all by the time the sun went down and he made a lot of money that day.

Growing up, Dad used me in his scams when he could. I can remember him teaching me at six years old how to steal his favorite carton of cigarettes (Pall Mall non-filters). He taught me to walk into the old Skaggs grocery store down on Vinton St. once a week with Mom and split away from her at the entrance, and then go over to where the brown paper sacks were from bagging groceries. From there, I would proceed over to the carton of cigarettes. I would pull a carton for Dad, slip it into the sack and then head out to the car. I put the sack into the car under the front passenger seat and would then go back in, find my mom and continue grocery shopping. If I was ever caught I was to say, "My mom always buys one; I was just getting it for her." After months of doing this solo I was to teach my sister Charity how it worked. As we were walking out, an undercover officer caught me walking out the door and grabbed the sack. He looked inside and saw the cigarettes.

We were so scared and just stared up at him not saying a word. He looked down and said, "Is your Mom here?" We nodded. "Well, you better go get her," he said. We ran around and found her and told her a guy stopped us. He took Mom into the back room and told her she was never welcome in this store again. She didn't talk to me about it and I remember being so scared for Dad to come home that night. When he did hours went by before he spoke to me. Finally he looked down at me with disappointment and all he said was, "I heard what you did today." Then Dad walked into the kitchen. He was disappointed in me at six years old for getting caught stealing his cigarettes the way he told me to steal them.

My earliest memories from that house are all of listening to them having sex. My Mom and Dad would have sex for 36 hours sometimes and I wouldn't get to see my Mom the whole time. He would always call her "a dumb fucking worthless cunt". Actually that was his go-to phrase for us all. Charity and I had been playing in our shared bedroom listening to them have sex for hours when he started yelling. Mom would beg, "Please Danny, don't!" I can hear the sounds and their voices today as I type this out. Then she would scream, he would beat her and she would wail and cry out loud. This happened every week in my childhood and I cried for my mother every single time.

My Father knew I was going to stand against him someday. The first sign of this was when I was swinging in the giant tree swing he made me. He was yelling at Mom when he looked up, yelled at me and told me "get off the swing and get my fucking ass down to the car now". But I kept swinging. He told me if I didn't do it he was going to kill me. I kept swinging anyways; he pulled out his gun and said, "If you don't get your fucking ass down here now I'm going to blow your fucking head off." I kept swinging as if I heard nothing. From at least 100 feet away and pointing the gun up at me, he shot the gun off. I kept swinging while he just stared at me. I paused for a moment then chose to get off my swing and come down. I didn't get punished and Dad would tell this story of defiance for years to come.

I think that is why he started beating me the most. It was around the same age of six years old when I can remember the two times in my childhood we got to have a malt from Dairy Queen. It was a big deal to us. Dad and Charity would share one, and then Mom and I would share one. We were sitting at the kitchen table and Mom passed me the malt for my turn. I was so excited I must have just started sipping as fast as I could through the straw before she would ask for it back. Dad saw something he didn't like, maybe it was my joy. He got up from his spot at the table walked over to me taking the malt from my little hands and poured it down my head and face. He put the cup on the kitchen table and walked out of the room. Charity and mom sat there frozen like statues. Then when it seemed safe Mom got up and cleaned me off. There was no explanation for this behavior from my Mom or my older sister.

Mom never explained Dad to us. She truly believed she was the only victim and that it would all work out one day. We would lay in bed with her and talk bad about Dad - she would say that he was an asshole and a jerk. Once we all took a magic marker and wrote bad things about Dad under the top bunk of our bunk beds. I loved my mom more than life itself. In my eyes, she was an angel being tormented by a monster.

Before I started kindergarten, my sister started to be mean to me; just little things at first so I would guess it was normal hate she had for me for just being born and taking any attention of Dad's and Mom's away from her. I can remember her always using me back then and trying to get me into trouble with Dad. She would pretend like she liked me to get close to me for a day and then find ways to hurt me. She was a little like Dad back then too, but different. We fought a lot.

Through the years, everyone would get snared into his trap of lies and manipulation. He would shine his gift of storytelling on them, and then reel them over to hang out as friends. Later that night he would have softened them up enough to take whatever he wanted from them and they would willingly sign their lives away to him.

CHAPTER 6: SHOOTOUTS AND SLEDGE HAMMERS

Our lives were a crazy roller coaster ride filled with intense moments. Dad had men and women all over town who wanted him dead. One day at Skaggs grocery store, two men walked in with sawn-off shotguns to kill Dad.

Dad and Tamera, Dan's sister, went to the grocery store to get some basics, when all of a sudden in walked two guys with sawn-off shotguns. They opened up their coats and pulled their weapons out, pointing them in Dan's direction. Danny threw the two brown paper bags of groceries he had in his arms straight up in the air and took off running to the back of the store. Tamera ran out the front door and got into her car to hide. Dan hid in the back and told the manager standing in the storage room to call the cops. The manager told him to leave and take his problems with him. Dad threatened the manager with his own life and then the guy called the cops. After the officers showed up Dad came out and found Tamera crying outside in the parking lot. The men had found her and left a message for her to tell Dan they were going to find him and kill him.

Years later at the Drive-in Theater over in Council Bluffs, Iowa, Mom and Dad left us on the swings because one of those guys showed up and parked his truck next to Dad. In his pick-up, sitting behind his head, was a mounted shotgun. Dad recognized the guy from Skaggs and slid down into the seat to exit the Drive-in. Mom came by later to pick us up, still swinging with no idea we could have been in a shootout.

Dad would ditch us as soon as something happened that put him at risk. He put money first, then himself, then his wife, and last his two kids. I wasn't even born yet when they were all in a head-on collision down in South Omaha. Charity, Mom and Dad were seated in the bench-style front seat of the old Chevy when they were hit. A young boy swerved into their lane, hitting them head on. Charity's little two-year-old head hit the dashboard and split wide open. Mom hit the windshield and when she came to and looked over, Dan was gone. This sums up most of who he was, always looking out for himself first. He probably had drugs and a gun on him with no license or papers. The girls went to the hospital and dad's sister Tamera came over to help out. I can remember getting into a car accident with him off of 42nd and Q St. and Dad cared more about the car and making sure he was in the right than he did to even see if I was OK. He spent ten minutes convincing the other guy it was his fault entirely and not my father's, before he took the second to look into the back seat to see if I was alright. He really cared about his cars and his possessions so much more than his own family. He wanted it all to look a certain way, even if it was really falling apart.

I was probably six or seven years old when Dad had all the guys from the slaughterhouse over the house on 18th St. There must have been a hundred guys hanging out, getting drunk and laughing. We were riding our bikes down on the street, in front of the stairs that lead up to our house, when a fight broke out.

Dad and his brothers had built a fort/deck in the front of our house the week before. It was about an 8-foot tall wall and made of wood, and it ran the width of the front of our house. From the street, it looked like a fort with tiny six-inch windows cut out for a rifle. Dad was a little paranoid because he had built up some enemies. Well, the city officials came during the week and told Dad he couldn't have it in his front yard. Nothing over six feet and it must be fifty percent see-through for city regulations of residential homes. Dad was pissed and planned to cut the legs off this giant fort and move the whole thing to the back of the house. To do that, he needed all the men from the slaughterhouse to come lift it; so, with the promise of a good time and free beer on a Saturday afternoon, and they all showed up.

When the City came back to see if Dad had complied, he pointed out the neighbor's fence across the street. He had a six-foot privacy fence and said that if he had to take his down then the neighbor had to take his down too. The City agreed and walked over to inform the neighbor of his misfortune. Now all our neighbors hated Dad anyway, because we would torture them. Dad would put dead animals at their doorstep and holler horrible things to them, especially when he knew they were going through something sad or traumatic. So this neighbor came out with a chainsaw, while all the guys were out front of our house, and started walking down his fence and cutting the whole thing in half.

Mom came down the front stairs to the street and got us off our bikes and took us inside. Then our neighbor got a sledge hammer and proceeded to knock every other board out of its place. He was pissed and he knew Dad had pointed him out to the city. Then, still pissed, he went into his house and came out with a handgun and started shooting into the crowd. Dad was standing there and saw no one was dropping from all the shots fired. He later said he was so excited because he realized he could legally kill somebody. Dad reached for the .38 Special Snub Nose he kept in the back of his blue jeans. At that same second Crazy Pauly pushed past Dad, knocking the gun from his hand and yelled, "I got him for ya, Dan."

You know you're a special kind of crazy when you work at a slaughterhouse in the 80's with five hundred of the meanest and toughest men and you're the one they all call "Crazy Pauly." His eyes pointed in two different directions and both were different colors. Tall and skinny with shoulder length blonde hair, I can remember he was crazy and always trying to impress my dad. So Crazy Pauly took off after this guy and chased this man into his home. You could hear gunshots and muffled yelling. After some time, the guy ran out the back door with Pauly hot on his heels. The neighbor was shooting over his right shoulder as he ran and popped Pauly in the leg. Crazy Pauly did a cartwheel in the air and fell to the ground. The neighbor went back into his house and the cops showed up – again.

Back then, Dad was always shooting guns off in our house. We had no basement, so he would just shoot right into the floor through the carpet. The crawl space under our home had a layer of bullets covering the dirt like a thick shag carpet. The cops would show up once a week and just ask through the door to see my Mom's face to make sure everything was OK. Dad would answer the door and make them laugh. They would ask, "Come on, Mr. Gardner. Can we just see Mrs. G's face and make sure she is OK?" Everybody just loved him and so did I.

Whenever there was a dull moment, he would do something that would shake the world around him up. He didn't like quiet, or normal, he wanted everything to go full-throttle, all the time. For instance, he stopped all the traffic on the interstate once; yep, that's how crazy he was. Now this is long before cell phones and Dad was driving in the car with my mom, Dad's aunt and her son. They had all just gone out to eat and Danny was trying to impress them. He said, "You guys want to see something cool?" Have you ever seen anybody stop the interstate before?" Danny spun the car doing cookies on the interstate until it slammed to a stop. He jumped out of the car and pulled out his gun, pointing it into all incoming traffic from both directions. Stopping all lanes of traffic, he yelled, "Ahhhhhhhhhhh," as he slowly spun in a circle pointing the gun at all the cars. He laughed and growled at the traffic, then got into his car filled with panicked passengers and drove away. His aunt never came over again.

CHAPTER 7: LAS VEGAS AND LOST TOES

We would spend our childhood begging Dad to stop the interstate again, or to get to go look at the prostitutes over in north Omaha. That was always a fun family past time. We would follow her with her John and then Dad would scare them while they were getting ready to have sex, causing the couple to flee on foot in separate directions. But the last time he did it, the guy jumped out of the car thinking we were the cops. He jumped out naked and we saw his pecker, so Dad said that was it - no more hookers. He always protected us from any sexual TV content or naked guys; I think this may have been the way he loved us and wanted to keep us safe. I laugh out loud now telling you that, but that's how it was. We always had to turn our heads watching horror films when the sex scene would come on.

Sometimes, Dad would also take us to St Joseph's Catholic Church on 16th St. Dad was an altar boy as a kid and I think he believed there was a God, so once in a while we would go and play church. I even went to ICM catholic school for two years by Stoysich Meats off 24th St. Sometimes we would skip church and Charity and I would just run in, put two dollars in the collection plate and then stick our fingers in the holy water so we could go to Orsis on 6th and Pierce St. They had the world's best freshly baked loaves of bread for a dollar and a quarter. We would tear into it and dip it in the butter we brought from home. Man, it was the best ...

We would drive around downtown, cross over the old South Omaha Bridge into Council Bluffs where we would hit the first gas station we came to, and Dad would spend hundreds of dollars on Pickles. It was great and he would get excited for a second when we would win; but he never walked away ahead, and always a few hundred dollars down.

He would then get mad and yell at Mom all the way home. I absolutely hated it when he would kick her out of the car. He would just pull over and kick her out. That was the worst feeling - looking out the back window at your Mom sobbing on the side of the road as your father drove off, leaving her with no purse and no way to get home. I hated Dad for it.

Back then, Dad was always betting everyone a hundred-dollar bill on something and it would sound like this: "Listen, mother fucker, I'll bet you a hundred-dollar bill you can't ..." and the person would bet against him. Who could punch themselves in the face the hardest and try to knock themselves out? Who could take a big enough bong hit and drop to the ground stoned? Who could run up and down our front stairs a hundred times for a hundred dollars? Could he drive his new Harley straight up the huge hill in our front yard on 18th St.? He lost that bet - he made it halfway up and rolled back down and lost a hundred dollars; then it was double or nothing and he drove that bike straight up our hill, but was going too fast and crashed into the back-side door of our home. He trashed his Harley and burned a huge hole in his leg. These things happened every day back then. It was very exciting, but it surrounded us with constant fear and pain.

We all went to the tattoo parlor to get Mom a tattoo on the inside of her upper right thigh that would read "Property of D.P.G." Charity, dad and I would wait out in the car while Mom went inside for a quick tattoo. I believe it was Ira's tattoo parlor on 24th Street. Dad parked the car and we just waited. A car pulled up behind us (blocking off an exit for an alley or a parking lot, I can't remember which) but this guy driving the car just sat there and stared at us. Dad asked, "Girls, what the fuck is this mother fucker doing behind me?" We turned around and I watched him bounce to his right across the bench seat and open the passenger door. I said, "I don't know, Dad, but he's getting out of the passenger seat." Then I saw he had a giant silver chain in his right hand. It was a tow chain and he had it circled up and dangling from his clenched fist as he was looking at us. He was swinging it around in circles on the side of his hip. Not like a helicopter blade above his head, but sideways along his body. He was nodding his head and walking in a way that said," Your mine now, mother fucker, I got you."

Of course, Dad threw our car into reverse and smashed that guy's legs between the bumper of our car and the bumper of this poor guy's car. I watched his arms go up and then saw him drop to the ground. As we raced away leaving my mom, I saw the guy rolling on the ground holding both of his knees to his chest. To me, this was just another awesome moment to tell people about. Mom was in getting a tattoo and the lady said, "Does your husband drive a silver Cutlass with tinted windows?" Mom said, "Yes". The lady said, "Well, you better get out of here because he just ran some guy over." So Mom ran out the back and wandered the streets looking for us. Charity and my dad's brother, Timmy, went back later to collect Mom. Eventually, she saw Charity's little fingers waving at her from Uncle Timmy's jeep

We ran away from Dad to Las Vegas once. Mom came running out of the house and grabbed us off the lawn. She said, "We're leaving your father, girls". Just so you know, every time we left Dad I was filled with joy, and every time he found us and talked her back into the house I was sad. I loved him, but he was batting fifty-fifty. Fifty percent of the time he was loud and funny, but the other fifty percent he was loud and trashing the house and beating us. It was a tough combination to deal with and there was no in-between.

We took the car and headed west. I can remember we stayed in a hotel where we stole the towels and soaps. We made it to Vegas, where my mom's older brother George lived and had agreed to take us in. It was like moving into the Brady Bunch house. I believe this was the first time I ever played with other kids. We roller skated and ran around the house like normal kids would. It was awesome and I felt we were safe and free from Dad. I was so happy and Dad was so far away that he could never find us. Mom told us why she had left. Dad had been drinking and getting high with his buddies. He had been trying to shoot a dime off his toe with a .22 pistol. Another bet that he could do it. He had been standing up, looking down his right arm, and balancing a dime off of his pinky toe. He had bet everyone in the house a hundred-dollar bill he could shoot the dime off the toe. He had already failed when Mom asked him to stop.

He looked up at her and in front of the guys said, "How much would it cost for you to get the fuck out of my life forever?" He tossed her five hundred dollars and told her, "Get the fuck out of my life and don't ever come back." So, like I said, things were awesome in Vegas. But back in Omaha, Dad shot his toe off that night. He kept flinching when he would pull the trigger so he had one-legged Donnie put his wood foot on top of Dad's foot so he might not flinch. He shot it off and the bullet even went through the toe next to it. He went to the hospital, then came back home to bet the boys who were still partying at the house, double or nothing that he could shoot a staple from a stapler off his bandages where his toe used to be.

The next morning dad called all the usual places to look for us, like Chris's dad's house, her Brother David's house, but no one was talking so he hired two detectives to find us. I don't remember how he found us, but before you knew it I walked into a bedroom in Vegas and saw Mom sitting on the bed, holding the phone to her ear and crying. Charity was standing in front of her. I was pissed as I knew what this meant and I knew we would be going back. I wasn't mad at Mom, I was just mad to go back to that house and back to Dad. I hated him now. I watched as Mom handed the phone to Charity; she was so excited to hear his voice at nine years old that she stood there and literally peed her pants. I walked out of the room not wanting to speak to Dad. By the next day, Dad was there passionately making out with Mom and then putting on the Dan show for everyone else, making them laugh at how stupid he had behaved and getting everyone to want to give him another shot because he was so funny and such a great guy.

We stopped at a casino before we left Vegas and Mom and Dad both went in, leaving us sleeping in the car. Dad played roulette, betting five-hundred-dollar bills; yes, he always had five-hundred-dollar bills on him. They exist; you just never see them because they are collected now. He was betting red and black on the table, just under a fifty-fifty shot to double your money. Dad lost thousands in just a few spins of the wheel. He screamed and yelled at Mom all the way home. Now when I say yelled, I mean he spit on her and hit her in her head. This happened the entire drive from Vegas to Omaha, saying things like, "You worthless two cent fucking bitch. If you ever pull this fucking shit again, I'll fucking kill you, I'll fucking kill you right fucking now. I will take a fucking gun and blow your Simple Simon-minded fucking brains all over this fucking car, you worthless dead cunt. Do you fucking hear me, you fucking dead cunt?" It plays so easily in my ears. It took a decade for his judgmental words to not play like a recording in my mind. When I walked into a room full of people, all I used to hear was all the negativity he had preached to me.

He quit drinking after that Vegas incident, because Mom had put her foot down. Dad would only do drugs and smoke pot from now on. The drinking made him the most violent and the most dangerous to himself and others. Dad would tell all these stories over and over through the years, using Mom as his punching bag when company was over at our house. She would get up from the table crying because he would go too far and they would all laugh. He would playfully call her back to the kitchen table and she would eventually come back out. If she didn't, she would get beat later when the company would leave and the Dan show was over.

Guns were a huge part of my childhood. Everywhere you looked in our home; there was a loaded gun on display. I had shot every caliber and type of gun by the time I was twelve years old. I was a great shot and so was my sister. I can remember pulling up to a bridge out in Nebraska with Dad when I was about ten years old and there was a guy laying down on the bridge sighting in his rifle. He was shooting at targets down in the gully under the bridge. Dad told me to go ask him if it was OK if I shot next to him off the bridge. I did and the guy said, "Yes." Dad opened up the trunk of our car to a hot arsenal of weapons. He pulled out the fully automatic Uzi and gave it to me. He said, "Let's scare the shit out of that guy. Go pull this trigger off next to him." So that's just what I did. The poor guy looked like he was about to have a heart attack, then stood up and asked, "What the hell is that thing?" I stood proud and replied, "It's my daddy's Uzi."

Dad was always looking to be aggressive, and sometimes this aggressiveness made him look like a Hero. Dad caught a purse thief once on 24th Street. Dad was pushed by a guy who ran passed him in a busy shopping crowd as a lady yelled, "Help, he stole my purse." Dad caught the guy in an alley and the guy looked at my Dad and just surrendered to him. Dad loved being a hero; he even got a letter from the City Mayor thanking him for being such an outstanding guy. You see how the lines of good and bad are drawn out so confusingly to describe who he was. I loved my Dad and thought he was the coolest person on earth, but I also wished him dead every day of my life.

CHAPTER 8: PICKLES AND PETS

I was in the second grade when we moved out of the house on 18th Street. Our next home was one block into Bellevue and was so clean and nice that we felt rich. I remember being mad at my dad because he made me leave my cat Whitefish behind and I cried silently for months. We felt like kings in our new home. Dad had hustled enough money for us to put a down payment on a house even though he was still making minimum wage at the slaughterhouse; I think it was about three or four dollars an hour. He marked our house with a huge wooden sign planted in the center of our lawn that read "Thee Gardner." It was about two feet tall by six feet wide and hung from a frame made of painted black four-by-fours. He wanted everyone to know that "There was only one Gardner," that was him and he was there to stay. He would still beat us and sometimes yell at us for three to four days at a time, but on the upside the parties slowed down. He wouldn't have the guys from the slaughterhouse over in big groups anymore.

I knew my dad had started doing cheap speed and coke and would make my mom do it too, "unknowingly". He would sneak it into her coffee without her knowing, but ten hours later she would figure out something was up because she was still wide awake and be mad at him. They would disappear into the bedroom to have sex for twenty-four hours at a time, while we had to listen to it all day and all night. Dad would give us money to buy stuff at Walgreens on 36th and Harrison, maybe because he felt bad. He would come out every few hours to check on us. He would be all slimy with baby oil and bug-eyed from the drugs. This happened from second grade until I ran away at eighteen years old. It was so gross for Charity and me. They would fight and have sex. Some of it was so horrible I can't even share it with you now. But my sister knows what we had to see and hear. I'm going to let a few things stay between us and silently bear those wounds with her. I've said enough.

I can remember him locking us in Charity's bedroom, telling us "Just lay in there and fuck ourselves all night". We were in second and fourth grade and I couldn't believe he would say such things to us. One night our puppy, a boxer named Rocky, pooped on the carpet and Dad woke us all up screaming at us. Mom was on her hands and knees in front of the huge piles of puppy diarrhea and Dad walked up to her with us kneeling by her side and he kicked that dog poop right into her face and hair. We sat next to her, crying and picking out the poop with our little fingers.

At one time, we had a Box turtle, a cat named Muffy and a Cocker Spaniel named Droopy. Dad came home one day and decided he wanted them all gone. He gave Mom an hour to get rid of them or he would kill them all. His outburst always seemed so random. He just came home and decided it when he looked down and saw pet hair on his pants. That was it - our pets we had had for a few years and loved with all our hearts were just gone.

We ran to a woman's shelter one day when Dad had lost his mind on us. It was over his dinner not being completely done when he got off work. We stayed there for a few days, but I remember mom lying on a couch with Charity nestled between her legs and they were talking. Someone at the shelter thought this looked weird and mentioned it to Mom. Mom took offense to it and the next thing you know we were in a hotel with the little bit of money we had. We sat up talking about our options and Mom said we had to go back. I took the 'hot' gold ring off my finger and begged her to pawn it so we wouldn't go back to Dad. She said. "We will see."

We went back the next morning and they had sex all day, then he mentally locked her in the bedroom closet all night. As he watched TV, he would turn his head to spit on her or would flick his cigarette butts at her. He would get up to hit her or just raise his fist to make her flinch. Dad even took his BIC lighter and threw it at her, hitting her and splitting open her forehead. She stood there quivering and bleeding until he said, "I'm sorry, go clean yourself up." She left the closet and the room and washed herself in the bathroom sink only to return and have him say, "You know what I ain't through with you - get back in the closet."

We even stayed away from him long enough to get an apartment once when I was in sixth grade. We were so excited but we had nothing, not even a pot to cook mac and cheese with. But that didn't matter because we were away from him. I was so happy. Unfortunately, we would have to go back to school and that meant Dad would be able to find us. I remember going to school that first day away from Dad. I had left my classroom in the middle of the day to go to the drinking fountain. I was walking down the hallway when I looked up to see my Dad walking towards me. I put my head down and knew this was it. I knew we would be going back home after school. Dad stopped me and started begging me to tell him where Mom was. I didn't hug him or cry. I just shook my head and said, "I don't know."

I truly had no idea so I said, "I will call her," and Dad followed me to the nurse's office to use the phone. I picked it up and in my sadness and fear I realized we didn't have a number because we didn't even have a phone yet. I told Dad this and went back to class so depressed. Dad didn't bother to try to woo me. I was un-wooable now. He had hurt us too badly for me to be swept off my feet by his charm and he knew I was done. When I went out of school, I found my mom and dad making out in the front seat of our car, parked right where all the students are let out. The windows were actually foggy from the long session of sucking each other's faces off. I opened the back door and just hopped in the back seat. Dad gave me a jar of pickles to eat for dinner when we got home and they went into their bedroom. I would then have to listen to them have sex all night long. I ate so many pickles I threw up pickles out my nose, giant salty chunks of pickles getting stuck in my nasal passages as I puked alone in the toilet.

I always thought for sure he was going to just kill us one day. I would daydream about taking one of the loaded guns lying around our house and just kill him. But I was so scared, it was a level of fear you just can't imagine. I don't remember what had happened, but Charity and I were sitting on her bed just listening to Dad yell like always; Mom was locked in her room and we were locked in Charity's. Dad got a gun and told us he was on his way to our rooms to kill us all. We knew we were going to die and I started to cry. I felt like I had let them down. Mom and Charity and I didn't want to die like this.

There was nothing we could do besides sit there and wait to get shot in the head by our dad. He was standing in the hallway and shot the gun - "bang." Then he started laughing like Woody Wood pecker on the cartoon: "uh uh uh uh uh ... uh uh uh uh uh ... auauauauauauauaua." BANG.

Another shot closer to our door then ... BANG. Another shot rang out. Charity and I just held each other and waited to die as Dad made his way to our bedroom door to kill us. I was in fifth grade and Charity was in seventh and we were going to be killed by our dad, but he never opened the door.

He pretended to kill our dogs a few times. He took a shot gun and pretended he shot my best friend Rocky, our boxer dog, in the back yard. I didn't find out until the next morning before I would go to school that he was alive. You might think you would have been strong enough to overcome this fear and tell a teacher. Well, I made it to the Principal's office once in fifth grade and she asked me what was wrong. All I could get out of my mouth was "my parents fight a lot." She said, "Honey, that's OK. All parents fight." Now by this point in time I had never seen anyone ever even try and stop my dad - not the cops, not family, not the neighbors, not one person. On two separate occasions, he chased her through the streets naked while she screamed and grown men would turn their heads to not get involved. So what could be expected of an eighty-pound daughter?

CHAPTER 9: SCAMS AND SCABIES

I remember starting to try to protect my mom the best I could about third grade. I would try to say things to get him to stop hitting her and hit me instead. I had grown pretty tough and was ready for him to stop saying he was going to "blow my fucking brains out" and would tell him to "just get the gun and do it." One day it hit an escalation as he was beating Mom downstairs. He looked up at me standing at the top of the stairs staring at him and he said, "What the fuck are you looking at?" I knew it was going to hurt, but he was dragging Mom by her hair across the floor, so with all the courage in the world I looked at my two hundred and twenty-pound, six-foot-one father and said, "FUCK YOU!". He took off like a speeding bullet up the stairs after me. I barely got my hand on the front door when he caught me.

I was in third grade at this time, when he slammed my head into the door frame and he picked me up and walked me to my room. He threw me overhand into the wall. I fell down and landed, sliding down in between my bed and the wall. I laid there motionless, too scared to move. He stared over me for a few seconds and walked out of the room. I felt like he threw me to kill me. I can remember laying on the hardwood floor once, after he had beat me, and taking my little fingers to write with my fingerprints "it was my dad who killed us." Just so the cops might find it. I can remember lying in bed praying and asking God to please kill my dad. "Please God, kill my dad." But I could still hear him beating my mom. Then one night I tried to make a deal with the Devil. Because if God was real and didn't want to help me, then I knew the Devil could. I pleaded in prayer: "To the Devil of this world, if you exist would you kill my dad right now, please. I would do anything if you would just do that for me." Nope, Dad was still alive and making his way to my room.

I was more like a boy by this time. I was picked on by my family for being dirty and having no teeth. I never showered or even brushed my teeth. I hardly ever went to the doctors. I even had tiny red bugs in my shoes. I caught the scabies, also known as the seven-year itch. It hurt so bad I would run my fingers through my hair just to cool the itch. This is a habit I still have to this very day. I felt like Charity was always favored by Mom and Dad. She would talk bad about me to the girls at school and make fun of me. My earliest memory of her, is when she and a girl making fun of me. We were taught to make fun of people in the worst way - to find out what they are most insecure about and verbally tear them apart for it. I learned how to do this well. It looked like, Charity was their favorite and they didn't bother hiding it. At Christmas, she would get a two-hundred-dollar stereo and I would get a Speak and Math. It would seem that Mom would always cater to Charity through the years and so did Dad.

Dad was layered in gold chains, bracelets and necklaces. Everyone at school called it the Mr. T starter kit. He wore a giant five-inch solid gold cross around a solid gold chain that looked like it was made for a large dog collar. Mom and Dad had gold and diamond rings they wore on every finger and never left the house without them - in fact they never took it all off. For the most part they had it on twenty-four/seven. Their gold and diamonds were their pride and joy and it was what they talked about the most, besides guns and sex. My sister had a goal and it was to also get covered in gold earrings, fingers, bracelets and necklaces. It was a gold frenzy. I can remember her always telling me she wanted to be covered in gold.

They seemed to treat her like a princess and I would feel picked on, mocked and laughed at. I felt like a verbal punching bag. Charity got straight A's in school until High School and I couldn't even begin to try to focus on my grades. She would also do-little things to get me beat by Dad or hurt me. One time, Dad lost a gun magazine and he tore the house apart, breaking everything we owned; when he found it, it was sitting on top of the pile he created in my room. She had found it and planted it in there. I was out digging through the trash outside when I heard him call my name. I got beat for it. This was not your normal sibling rivalry.

She was so beautiful; I can remember every boy in the neighborhood having a crush on her. But our relationship as sisters was sabotaged by Dad at birth. Dad would talk horribly about Mom to us, calling her a whore and telling us how stupid she was. He made fun of her all day every day. He would say, "Ain't that right Chris?" and if she didn't answer, "Yes, that's right ", fast enough she would be in trouble. She didn't even know what he had said half the time as she rushed to answer. When I would leave the room, he would tell Charity any dirt he knew on me and they would talk bad about me, saying how stupid I was and how dumb any decisions I was making in life were. Then I would walk into the room and Charity would walk out to do something and Dad would tear her up, saying awful stuff about the things she was doing and the way she looked. He kept all of us hating each other and loving only him.

Mom wasn't allowed to even be friends with us for too long. Sometimes he would be mad at me and no one in the house would talk to me for a week because he would convince them to not talk to me, or they were just scared to. They would both give me a nose-turned-up-in-the-air look as if I was Cinderella and they were the evil stepsisters. It was awful having Dad treat you like garbage, but when your mom and sister had to hop on board it was ten times worse. I grew wise to this at a young age and would try telling my sister what Dad was doing to us. I can remember even at 24 years old trying to tell her that Dad was using her and sabotaging her relationship with her husband. I would tell her only a little of what he was doing and saying behind her back because I knew saying too much was going to hurt her. She would say it didn't matter because she only wanted him to love her and she loved him no matter what, even though it was obvious that Dad was destroying Charity's marriage and her finances for his own personal profit and sick fun. Unfortunately, even though we knew his ways, we would all eventually fall back into the same trap, just looking for his love and attention.

Dad had quit dealing in hot stuff when we moved on up to Bellevue. He also quit loan sharking, but would still scam every poor sucker that walked through our front door. He would get them to fall in love with him by telling his stories and spoiling them with attention. I loved how Dad would leap from his seat and grab them to get them involved with his crazy tales. He was just so animated and entertaining and they would laugh their asses off. But then Dad would notice a ring they were wearing and by the end of the night cut a deal that they would not benefit from.

He would find out what they had that he wanted. Boats, guns, cars, motorcycles, diamonds, even Rolexes - whatever they had worth money, Dad would eventually end up with. Everyone had a price tag on their heads, including me. Let's just say if you walked in our door and you had a nice boat worth five thousand, by the end of the night the boat would be in our driveway with the bill of sale saying five hundred, for tax purposes, with a verbal promise of six thousand more tomorrow. I don't care how smart you think you are - every doctor, lawyer, and Indian Chief who walked into our house walked out ripped off and was never heard from again.

As I got older, I would beg Dan's own sisters not to do any money deals with Dad. And within a week one was back out of our house with her wedding ring on my mom's finger. It was disgusting and I was, mostly unwillingly, in on it all. It made me so mad, but I had no choice but to cooperate and do what Dad told me to do. They wouldn't just get snared into his trap once, sometimes it was over and over again. There was no bottom for how low he would stoop. He had us collect money for charities and keep it all. But this was how we got basic school clothes, so we were excited to do it.

The worst one was when Dad's lifelong friend was swindled into buying him a car. His name was put in good faith on the title and he promised to pay her every month. He paid her maybe a few times and soon quit talking. To butter her up about one week before the swindle, he took his lifelong friend over a shoe box. He told her that inside was personal items he wanted to give to Christine and the girls should anything ever happen to him. Dad told her he trusted her to take care of it if he should die of a heart attack. I saw what he put in there as he laughed out loud because of the genius of his plan - one old VHS tape and a rock for weight with some crumpled up papers for sound. He thought it was hilarious and when he took it to her house, he stole her video recorder on the way out the door. When she mentioned days later someone stole it, Dad blamed her own kids or even the kid's boyfriend who he was sure he saw over there. Dad was a horrible friend too.

CHAPTER 10: TOUGH GUYS AND TATTOOS

We would often go to Fontenelle Forest just before dusk to see the deer - it was Dad's favorite car cruise. We returned one night and, as I went into my bedroom, I heard a loud crashing noise from outside. I looked out my bedroom window and a car had come down our street and crashed into the cars parked in our neighbor's driveway. I told Dad, "Someone just hit the neighbor's cars across the street." Dad looked out the window and saw a guy two houses down running away from the scene. Dad took off out the front door; he was the fastest man I've ever seen on foot. I went outside to find our neighbors were hysterical. Whoever had hit their cars was long gone, but so was my dad.

A few minutes went by and, just like the unsung hero he was, I saw my dad come walking up the street. He was out of breath and holding this guy by his arms, twisted behind his back. My neighborhood, who had all hated dad, erupted in cheers! Tonight he was a hero and that hero yelled, "Danny Marie! Go inside the house and get my handcuffs." Like a bullet, I took off and was soon assisting my dad in handcuffing this guy to the door handle of his own car. Dad always had a way to make you feel so cool along with him. Before the cops came, Dad took the guys weed, acid and money out of his wallet, as a favor for the kid of course. And when the cops showed up again, it was me who had to go get the keys for the cops so they could take the cuffs off the perpetrator. We were heroes for a night, Dad and me.

Our neighbors didn't talk much to us. I remember Charity and I throwing our make-up at one of our neighbor's windows, trying to get them to call the cops one night when we thought Dad was going to kill us all. Their kitchen light turned on, then off again, but I know they could hear the gunshots. I would sit in our back yard or look out my bedroom window at our neighbor's homes and wish they would let me come live with them. I even used to daydream about any of our neighbors calling the cops on my Dad. Our windows were open and anything my Dad said and yelled through all those years would echo through the whole neighborhood. But not one single time did any of them call the cops. I am disappointed in them till this day. They heard my mom scream and heard the guns being shot, but they were "mind your own business kind of neighbors". Every one of them knew bad things were happening in our home and they did nothing. Were they too scared to anonymously call the cops? Or did they just think it was none of their business?

A guy tried to kidnap Charity once. Charity was a very tall and beautiful girl whose looks took after the Gardner side of the family. The Gardner girls are all tall and stunningly beautiful in my eyes. You should see all my aunts; they are timeless beauties. At the age of twelve, Charity already looked sixteen years old. The boys in the neighborhood would try to sneak peeks of her through her bedroom window. One sunny summer day, Charity was going to cut the grass and in order to do that she was going to need to go get gas from the station two blocks up. She took our dog, Rocky, with her as Dad always ordered and headed to the gas station.

Halfway there, a car pulled over and a guy opened the passenger door and said to her, "Hey, let me give you a ride, where you going?" Charity was so scared she didn't answer. He continued to follow and told her, "Come on, get in the car. I'll give you a lift." Charity just kept walking and finally the guy called her a "fucking bitch", and took off upset. Charity was too scared to tell anyone what happened because Dad was always mad at us for looking too old. We couldn't cut our hair or wear make-up. He was very controlling. Our hair was all one length and we couldn't even tuck it behind our ears. So Charity came home and told me, then Mom told Dad. Luckily, Dad wasn't mad at Charity, nor did he try to find an angle to blame her for what had happened.

Dad's Uncle Jim and Aunt Pat lived in our neighborhood and were still friends with Dad at the time. Jim was a good old boy who believed in family and justice. Dad called Jim and told him the scoop, and had him keep his eyes out for a guy matching the description. Pat and Jim lived one block away and owned rental properties in our neighborhood. We pulled out our driveway that same day to go somewhere. Our house sat in the middle of the block on the side of a small hill with a slight incline. We pulled out with our car's back end facing up the hill to head down the street. As Dad put the car into drive from reverse, he made eye contact with the guy driving up the street. The guy looked at Dad, and then looked at Charity sitting in the back seat with me and his eyes got huge. Charity yelled, "That's him, Dad! That's the guy!" Now I had seen some cool things in my childhood, but this was the coolest thing I had ever seen. My Dad threw that car in reverse and headed uphill backwards and parallel to that guy and pointed at him and yelled, "You mother fucker, Yeah, you!" That guy floored it and so did my dad. It was a side by side race up the street. Now, at the top they both had to make a slight turn to the left as both cars raced towards Harrison St., just off of 42nd. Dad was going faster backwards then the guy next to us was going forward. Then, right in front of Pat and Jim's house, Dad spun a half cookie, blocking the street off with his car just ahead of the guy. The guy had to slam on his brakes and Dad jumped out and ran after his car.

The guy threw his car into reverse as Dad made it to his driver's side window. Dad smashed the guy's cigarette into his face and grabbed him by the throat with his left hand. Dad wasn't going to be able to keep up on foot so he reached his right hand over the steering column for the keys. I was so excited because Dad was going to kill this guy. The car gained speed going in reverse, and Dad ran alongside in his leather sandals. He had his finger on the keys, but the guy picked up too much speed and was able to shift forward and cut up the side street. Dad came back to our car and I hung my head out to see his sandals. The sides of his leather-sewn and braided sandals had blown completely out. It was nutty. We went home and Dad decided to call the police. The cops came to the house and we all filed a police report.

Later on that night, we got the call from Jim. He had found the car in our own neighborhood and he came by to get Dad and take care of it. Dad had said that he and Jim went with intentions to kill the guy. But there in the car outside this guy's place, they discussed their options. I don't know who decided that it was a bad idea to kill anyone, probably Jim, but they decided to just call the cops and let them handle it. The cops showed back up later after talking to the guy. The kid was young and the cops partially took his side, saying Charity looked much older than what she was, and the kid was an idiot who was now scared to death. He was trying to flirt with her and thought she was much older and stuck up because she wouldn't say hi to him. Dad agreed with the cops' view and let it go. The kid moved out of our neighborhood and sent Charity a bouquet of flowers with an apology note.

That's why Dad was so strict with us. We both turned out to be head-turners, so Dad wouldn't even let us leave our back yard growing up. The boys in our neighborhood called our back yard our playpen. I didn't mind it so much, because it was about a half an acre and Dad always had a moped or a go-cart for us to play with. He even built us a ramp for the carts, plus one summer he took four railroad ties and a drum and built us a bronco bull to ride. He put the four ties into the ground with cement and hung a fifty-gallon drum off chain in the center of the four posts. It all sat about two feet off the ground. He attached some bull horns to the drum and a saddle to sit on. We had our own "mechanical" bull when you pulled on the chains in front. I remember our fence line being lined with boys to watch us play with our cool toys.

Unfortunately for me, the overprotective and strict thing was way out of order. I wasn't allowed to sit on the couch in our front room until I was thirteen years old. I had to know what Dad wanted when he snapped his fingers or get hit in the back of the head. I never got to go to a single football game or pep rally. I went to one dance in seventh grade and was never allowed to go again. I never went to any homecoming, prom, or track meet. I was not allowed to cut bangs on my hair until seventh grade or shave my very hairy legs. I was not allowed to take any sports or even photography. Despite all this, I managed to have a few girlfriends through the years. One I had in second grade was named Becky, and then there was Cori in fifth and sixth. I actually got to spend the night over her house a few times. But I was a weird and confused little girl. I didn't know if I liked girls or boys, I just knew I wanted to be cool like my dad and do drugs and have lots of sex. Dad told me once he slept with a new girl every weekend and that's what I wanted to do to. Girl or boy, I couldn't wait to get started. All I thought about was drugs and sex at this point in my childhood.

My Uncle Timmy had moved in with us when I was twelve years old and in the seventh grade at Bryan Jr. High. I went into the new school year with no friends. I was the girl who would wear all black and give squinted eye looks to everyone. Unfortunately, the squinted eye look was because I needed glasses and didn't know it, so everyone thought I was giving them dirty glances all the time. The first day in the cafeteria, a girl came up to me and told me that "so and so said you called her a bitch and she's going to kick your ass." I had no idea who 'so and so' was and I had no clue what to do with this new information. It seemed like every tough girl in Jr. High was threatening to kick my ass. I was a pretty girl despite my all black scary look, and I remember this popular boy named Larry who I thought was cute. We kissed behind the football field, and then I had all these girls named Tina who were threatening to kick my ass because of it. I was physically fighting with a giant crazy dad at home so these girls didn't stand a chance. But if I got into trouble at school, I knew what my father would do to me at home. I finally went to a counselor to plead with one of the girls to stop. "My father will kill me if I get in a fight at school," I remember telling her. She eased off and so did the other girls.

I finally made friends with the stoners. The stoners dressed like 1980's rock stars and smoked cigarettes in the woods before school. I was already smoking pot every day and had tried the leftover cocaine left on the table by my family. It was no big deal to start smoking cigarettes.

My uncle Timmy had been living in our basement for a few months now. He was my favorite; because he would get me high before school every day and then when I got out of school we would smoke more pot and shoot pool in the basement. Timmy was a tall, skinny crack and heroin addict who was momentarily clean. He had scammed every person he had ever met, including his own children. He would steal their identities and rob them blind. He was a sick man. His stories were wild and crazy and for some reason I held a special place in his heart always. He treated me like an adult and we would just hang out together, laughing and talking. He was kicked out by Dad within a year.

I was eleven, turning twelve, when Guns and Roses played on the radio and was my favorite band in the whole world. I then decided I wanted a tattoo. Now my dad and mom both had a few tattoos, so I decided to ask my dad if I could get one. He said no. Then the first and only time I played sweet on my dad, one week before I turned twelve, I talked him into it. Dad was sitting on the couch in his resting spot only he was allowed to sit in and I heated up a can of Hormel chili in the microwave and took it out to him with crackers. I said, "Dad, I turn twelve next week and no guy I end up marrying will even care whether or not I have a tattoo. It doesn't even matter to anyone. Can I please get a tattoo?" He said, "Fine, have your mother take you tomorrow, but it can't be larger than a quarter and it must be somewhere where your swimsuit covers it up - and no skulls or daggers." "Deal," I said excitedly, as I gave him a big fat hug and kiss.

So there I was at the tattoo parlor on 24th Street, a quarter in my hand and going along the wall, slowly eyeballing the size of each tattoo compared to my quarter. In seconds, I chose a rose and got it placed on my right hip. It was the best day ever and I couldn't wait to go to school and show it off. I wore sweatpants for a month so I could easily pull them down to show everyone my new tattoo.

I don't remember much about what type of person I was back then. I can remember a few teachers thinking I was going to kill someone and pulling me out of class to check if I had a weapon on me. I remember a female teacher bullying me and making me cry in class once. In seventh grade, I was stealing white crosses from my dad and taking them to school to share with my friends. It is a little white pill, also called cheap speed. I would pass them out for free to whoever wanted them. I was allowed to attend my seventh-grade dance, and I took track practice for two days, but knew Dad would never take me to the meets. He would convince me I didn't want to or I was not cut out for it and so I just didn't do anything. I would make a suggestion to try tennis or track and he would say, "What the fuck do you want to do that shit for?" He would tell me it was too much money or I wouldn't be any good at it and completely shut the door on me trying anything. It's a shame, because I had so much athletic potential. So I just did drugs and chased boys.

CHAPTER 11: BAD GRADES AND BAD HAIR

My grades were always awful. I would try to focus in school but it seemed impossible. Charity was a straight A student until ninth grade. I can remember sitting down with her for help with assignments, but we would both agree it was easier and faster for her to just do my homework for me. She was two years older than me, and hated spending time with me. She was very cruel to me and would try anything to get Dad mad at me or have him be mean to me. Charity would always bully me. She would have her friends make fun of me. One of my youngest memories is of her ditching me to cry in the aisle at the grocery store, only to get in trouble from Dad. She pretended to like me if it made her look like a kind older sister to anyone who was watching.

I was the one Charity called Pigpen because I was so dirty up until seventh grade. I had scabies, bugs in my shoes and had rarely showered in my life. Seriously, I would walk into the shower to get wet and then walk right back out. I must have smelled something awful. But that summer I had grown pretty, and boys started to notice me. I remember going to the swimming pool right before Junior High and seeing these boys, the Newquest brothers, who were the cutest boys I had ever seen up to that point. For the first time ever, boys were flirting with me; Charity seemed to get mad whenever I got attention. If my mom or dad showed me any attention, Charity would throw a temper tantrum. And in order to keep her content, they would just not give me attention or affection in front of her.

So Dad would be mean to me in front of Charity, calling me names and making fun of me because it made her feel special. The favoritism had me wishing I was dead most of my life. It's hard on a kid growing up being the black sheep. I didn't fit into my family and lucky for me they kept pushing me out. Charity and I would laugh and have a great time together and she would walk into the house telling Mom and Dad how horrible it was to be with me.

I felt like I did not belong anywhere, not with my family or the whole world, it felt like I was the only one who could see who they really were and I was so alone. How could I be the only one who thought my family was crazy - the only who thought they were awful people and only out for themselves? I hated the way they treated people; how they sat around and talked bad about the people who were just sitting in front of them and were treated like a best friend two seconds before; high fiving each other over what they could scam off of a person.

Every day my mom would pick us up from school, the very first thing I would ask her was, "Is dad in a good mood or a bad mood?" If she had blood on her face or a torn shirt, spit in her hair or just started crying, I knew I would be walking into anywhere from an hour to thirty-six-hour session of Dad freaking out on us all. One year, I came home with the same below grade averages: one A, two B's, three C's, and an F or two. Charity had also gotten bad grades, so Dad ordered Mom to take us and have our hair cut off as a punishment. At this time, I was in eighth grade and finally allowed to have bangs, but I was not allowed to get my haircut from being very long; so this was a shock to both Charity and me. We came home from school and Mom drove us to the hair salon right next to the Captain Video we would walk to. Charity and Mom had gotten into a screaming match and I remember Charity treating Mom like Dad does, calling her an idiot and telling her things like, "Dad is right about you." So Mom took us and as we sat there Charity stood up in protest and said to me, "They can't do this to us. Come on, Danny." So Charity and I walked out of the hair salon and walked to her friend Amber's house, which was two or three blocks away. We hid out for a few hours, and when Dad got home from work we went home.

I remember Dad absolutely losing his mind on us. We were spanked bare bottom and he took scissors and cut our hair off to our earlobes. It was an awful experience for me. I already knew Dad was insane from when, a few months prior, he found a note a boy had written to me and made me sit at the kitchen table and literally eat it. I looked at him that day and through tears told him, "You really are crazy." We had little white shoes, like Keds, that were popular with all the girls in school. Dad didn't like them on our feet, so when I got out of school, my dad took my shoes and threw them out the window, right there in front of Bryan Jr. High.

The list of things Dad would get mad about was so long and changed regularly. The worst was when the sink would back up or the car would get a scratch. I remember we were all in the car once on 36nd and Q St. There was a bank on the corner and Dad had to use a bank card for the first time to withdraw money. I was in the back seat with Charity, and Mom sat frightened in the passenger seat. We were going camping that weekend at Platte River State Park in Nebraska. Dad pulled up to the automated teller, but the sun was shining and he couldn't read the prompts. Dad couldn't work the machine and so he started yelling at Mom and then he just put the car in drive and gunned it while screaming at us all. Mom said, "You gotta go back; you left the card in the machine." Dad slammed on his brakes and the car behind us smashed into our rear end. Dad jumped out screaming and scaring the crap out of the guy who hit us. The impact was so strong that when the car was hit the trunk popped open. Unfortunately for Dad, there was weed in the trunk as well, so he ran out and slammed it shut. Dad never checked on us to see if we were hurt. The cops came and everything worked out to Dad's advantage like always.

Dad lost an ounce of his weed once. Now an ounce is a fair amount of weed; that is exactly how much weed my dad smoked about every ten days. A hundred and twenty dollars an ounce was the going price at this time and Dad lost his bag. I remember him going room to room while we stood and cried, watching him as he broke our furniture and tore down every picture and shelf in the house for hours. Later, he was in the kitchen screaming and calling us "whores and cunts" like always, as we were frantically looking all over. Mom was on her knees crying and looking through the trash, and I was looking into the kitchen when I saw my dad open the refrigerator. He looked in the side door and pulled out his weed, then looked over his right shoulder at Mom who was weeping over the trash all over the floor. Dad immediately took the pot and dropped it back behind the microwave. When your pot gets dry, you can put an orange peel in the bag and put it in the fridge so it won't burn too fast later. That's what Dad had done and forgot he had done it.

He yelled, "I found it, right fucking here, right where one of you worthless fucking cunts knocked it off the microwave and made it fall back behind." Of course I called him out and said softly, "No you didn't, you found it in the fridge and threw it behind the microwave." He sent me to my room and it was never mentioned again. Dad was a compulsive liar but always said; "Only one thing I hate in this world is a liar." He would also quote Scarface: "I only got two things in this world - my word and my balls - and I don't break them for no one." Just like his behavior, this never made any sense.

Mom ran away over and over again, sometimes leaving Charity and me to hang around to hear Dad call everyone he knew and say, "Yeah, the bitch fucking left me again." Then he would get a hold of Mom and fake cry to her and beg her to come home. It was disgusting. Dad could convince everyone over and over again. He even convinced Charity to drop out of high school in the three days while Mom was gone by saying. "Charity, I need you to take care of things for me now that Mom is gone. Char, I can't read - how am I gonna pay the bills? I need you to stay home and take care of me and the house." She was in eleventh grade when he convinced her he would lose the house if she didn't take over paying the bills and grocery store duties. He also convinced her to get engaged to Chuck, her boyfriend at the time, and the two of them would just live in the house together paying Dad rent. So they did.

I looked up to Charity, but I could never figure out why she always hated me back then. She would have fun with me outside, and then go back in and tell mom and dad how awful it was to hang out with me because I was embarrassing or an idiot. I never understood why, but it hurt so badly and I never stopped trying to be her friend.

My mind was full of my father's distorted, negative opinions of everyone and everything. Most people can walk into a room filled with other people and have their own thoughts and go have conversations with those around them. Unfortunately, when you grow up in a home like mine all you hear is the most powerful voice you grew up with and you think those are your own thoughts playing in your mind; I eventually learned that they are not.

For a moment, imagine you are walking into a high school dance at eighteen years old. You would see friends, notice the decorations, possibly smile at the song being overplayed, and maybe make your way to a table of people you know. When you have been raised by someone like my father, you walk into a room and your head is filled with their negative voice playing like an old record about everything you notice. This is what it sounded like for me: "Look at that stupid mother fucker over there. I bet he's gonna stand there all night because nobody here even likes his dumb ass. And she is so fucking fat I don't even know why she would show up. Look at her she - can't even afford a fucking dress. Look how ghetto she looks, fucking ghetto bitch. She can somehow afford to get her fucking nails done, but can't afford to lose weight." I know it sounds horrible, but it's all you hear. I know this is true because it happened in my head for years. It was Dad's negative voice playing like a record in my head, mocking and laughing at everyone in the room - even our own friends and family.

Charity would tell me several times about the voices in her head and I would explain to her what was going on; that it was Dad's overpowering voice repeating all this crap he shoved on us over and over. Unfortunately, I believe our relationship was so tarnished by our father that she could never respect or receive anything I could offer her in terms of advice.

Crazy passed from my father's father, to my father, to my sister and me. I pray it ends there and even reverses the process one day so my sister can be free from Dad too.

CHAPTER 12: BAD MOODS AND BULLET HOLES

Dad almost seemed immortal to us, because everyone feared him and no one ever stood too strongly against him. But one day that all changed when I was fifteen years old and Charity would have been seventeen or eighteen at the time. Dad was in a car accident at forty years old and won a huge lawsuit where he would get so much every month and then started to collect social security ... forever. He wasn't really hurt, but he sure put on a show for the judge. Dad walked in that courtroom with reading glasses on and a cane. The prosecutors were watching our house for months trying to catch him looking active and uninjured. He would go knock on their van to let them know he could see them. He won a few false lawsuits through the years, but this lawsuit put him home twenty-four hours a day and seven days a week. He even bought a custom-made black baseball hat that said "Retired." He really felt like a success story. He was in the best mood ever and we were all going to go out that evening to celebrate. He called Charity and me on the answering machine, because we were still never allowed to answer the phone. Through the machine he said, "I'll fucking tear your head off if you don't answer this fucking phone right now. OK cock suckers, we're going out so get your fucking asses ready. Your mother and me will be home later to pick you bitches up!"

Now I know it is hard to believe, but we were so excited that Dad was going to be in a good mood for the first time in a long time. This was the happiest I had ever heard him in my life. That message was how he talked to us all the time, but this time it was a great thing. Chuck, Charity's fiancé, was living with us so he was coming to. Charity and I went and got all dolled up because Dad was coming to take us out. Going out anywhere with Dad was always a blast when he was in a good mood and right now he was in the best mood ever! Hours went by and we sat around the kitchen table at the house on 39th Street, staring at the phone with no word from Mom and Dad. We were impatiently waiting for something to happen. Finally, the sun went down and my parents' car pulled up, and so we ran outside to greet them. Mom leaped out of the car crying out loud and ran into the house, holding the left side of her face. Our hearts fell, like usual, as she darted past us to hide in the house. As I got older, she would sometimes come into my room to hide behind me and I would just stand there as he yelled at her past me. When he would hit me, it would turn into an unfair fight that must have made him feel awkward - equivalent to Hercules fighting Cinderella (at least that's how it felt). But even outweighed by a hundred pounds, I would still claw at him and charge him with all I had.

We all scurried into the house like little frightened mice. Dad went on a rampage screaming, "This fucking bitch ain't sexy no more, and doesn't show enough tit. She is a worthless fucking cunt who ain't good for shit and I should just kill her right fucking now! You are all a bunch of worthless fucking sponges and every single one of you can go finger fuck yourselves!" Yep, that's my dad speaking to me saying the same things since I was born. In the screaming, I was able to piece together that they had picked up the cash driving around from bank to bank, because one bank wouldn't give out that much money in one transaction. Then they made their way to the titty bar over in Council Bluffs to party. That's where Dad started drinking and who knows what happened from there to now ... but it wasn't good.

Mom was quivering and hyperventilating at the kitchen table and I went down the hall to cry in my room and listen to him yell about her and us. After about five minutes, Dad yelled, "Danny Marie, get your worthless fucking ass out here and go out to the car and get my gun." I know to you this sounds insane. My dad had loaded guns all over the house all the time. He always had a loaded gun on him, and he always forgot one in the car every time he left the house and it had been my job as his daughter to go and retrieve his gun my entire life.

I felt some hope the argument was going to die down at this point because of the way he shouted at me. It sounded slightly rational. So I jumped up and went out to the car like I had many times before and got Dad's gun. The .38 snub nose revolver was right where he always left it, tucked under the driver seat. I got it and went back inside, passing Charity and Chuck who were on the front stairs smoking a cigarette. They also thought nothing of this as I walked past them with a gun. I walked in and set it on the kitchen table and went back to my bed to sit it out. As long as he was not up from his chair, Mom was not getting hit and it would slowly settle down.

Just as my butt touched the bed, "BOOM"! The gun went off and I leaped to my feet and ran out to the kitchen. Dad shouted, "Yeah, I shot at the bitch and she's lucky I didn't fucking kill her." The front door opened and Charity and Chuck were standing there wide-eyed. Charity screamed, "Did you just shoot at mom? You can't shoot at my mother!" Dad yelled, "Get the fuck out of my fucking house and don't ever come back! You don't ever fucking come back here, you fucking bitch." Charity screamed through tears, "You can't shoot at our mother," and she and Chuck ran out the front door.

Our kitchen table sat up against the wall in our tiny green kitchen. Mom's chair was on one side and Dad's on the other, both with their backs against the wall. Dad had raised the gun and shot at Mom at point blank range right through my mom's huge curly black hair. The bullet landed into the side wall directly behind the top of her head. I knew he just did it to scare her and make her cry more, so I sat down at the kitchen table between them. Now the fight was serious and was going to last hours and he might hit her. Dad stood up and I stood up. He came around the table and I placed myself standing in front of Mom, who remained seated with her head down. He was really wound up and he started to throw punches at her around me as I faced him, just enough to connect with her head a few times and make it hit the wall behind her. I stepped forward and Dad backed up. "You worthless fucking cunt," Dad yelled at me. "You good-for-nothing jack-yourself-off, cock-sucking bitch, I oughta fucking just kill you right fucking now. I oughta just blow your fucking brains out all over this fucking floor." I told him firmly, "Just do it then, get the fucking gun and blow my fucking brains out."

He just kept yelling and the phone rang. It was a female officer and I watched as the floor fell from under my father's feet. Charity and Chuck had stopped at a gas station and at that same time there were a couple of cops standing outside their cop car. Charity mustered up the courage that I could never find to tell them what was going on in our home. She must have been terrified to go against our father even at that age. The phone rang and it was a police officer. Dad went into panic mode as his eyes were the size of silver dollars. In a whirlwind of decision making, Dad made me answer the phone, usually because the call was always picked up through our answering machine, so we all heard her voice at the same time. Dad then had me hide the bullet hole with a wooden peg and hang a kitchen towel on it so it would look like a towel holder. The officer wanted to talk to Mom so I handed the phone to Mom, who was hyperventilating through tears and couldn't speak.

Dad dropped to his knees in front of her and started begging. "Oh, Krissy please baby, please. I'm so sorry, don't let them take me to jail, Krissy. Baby, please don't let them take me to jail." Mom couldn't speak through the tears and the officer told her to tell Dad he needed to step outside with his hands held up. Dad and I looked through the kitchen blinds into the backyard and under the cover of night I saw cops everywhere. They were hopping fences and crawling on their bellies towards our house. The front of our house was lit up like a Christmas tree from the cop cars pointing at it from every direction. I was so excited something was going to happen and thankful that someone had called the cops.

Dad walked to the front door and started yelling, "Don't shoot, don't shoot!" and started ripping all his clothes off yelling, "I ain't got a gun. Don't shoot!" I walked out with him and watched Dad strip down to his BVD whitey tighties in front of the cops. He never stopped pleading with them to not shoot him as they loaded him up and took him off to jail.

The cops came in and found the bullet hole with help from Charity, who recognized a new peg holding a dog towel on the wall that she had never seen before. They started talking to Mom when Charity and Chuck came in and I realized it was been Charity and Chuck who had called the cops for us. There was a woman who came in, dressed in street clothes, that talked to us all and asked questions. Charity and I sat on the couch as the cops slowly searched the house. Charity looked over and asked me, "Should we tell them about Dad's guns?" I nodded my head and so we stood up and told the cops that hidden behind the large picture was the gun he had used that night, and all Dad's other weapons.

When you slid the huge picture frame, it revealed a secret hidden wall and a beautiful arsenal of weapons that lit up with lights installed inside the wall - all chrome and gold inlaid guns. Some were for shooting and some were just for looking at. Charity and I decided together we would just tell the truth and let the cards fall where they may on Dad. We filled out police reports of exactly what had happened that night in full detail. The officers started to take down Dad's guns and toss them into a large bag. I could hear them banging and scratching against each other and could only think of Dad freaking out when he got out of jail over his guns being scratched. I told the officers which guns were loaded and even told them how to remove the clip on Dad's 9mm Uzi. Mom had us take all the cash, a brown trash bag full, up to our Uncle Jim's house so the cops wouldn't find it and take it. We came back and I told the officer I was going to stay with my sister over at her boyfriend's parents that night. I didn't want to stay with Mom and have her cry over Dad getting arrested all night long. I wanted to go with Charity, because I could smoke pot and cigarettes over there.

The next day, we came back home and Mom was doing everything she could to bring Dad home. She was on the phone with him and the lawyers all day long. Charity had moved in with Chuck's family and Dad was back home in two days. The second before he came home, a cop car pulled up and took me to jail. They put me in a holding cell with boogers and blood all over the walls. No one told me what was going on; I just went because they told me to. They then took me to a house somewhere in Omaha where I got signed in and sent to a room. It was a youth home for troubled teens. These kids were weird, dirty and crazy. That night I slept in a room full of other girls and listened to the girl in the bed next to mine masturbate all night long. It was awful, and I did not want to be there at all. The next morning my Aunt Jamie called me and I remember saying, "Please come get me." She arrived within thirty minutes and I was out of there.

CHAPTER 13: SUICIDE AND SLAUGHTERHOUSES

Dad was home with Mom, and I was now living with my Aunt Jamie in a nicer part of Omaha. Jamie had a one-year-old son named Kyle, and her husband at that time was Perry. These months would become the best time of my life. I was in tenth grade and Jamie would let me have a girlfriend over to spend the night like it was no big deal. She would let us go roller skating and she would even give me spending cash. Perry even let me help him fix a deck off the back porch. I had done many projects through the years with my father, but was always on edge, because at any minute, those projects could turn south and they always did. But I remember we talked during the project and Perry treated me like an adult with an opinion that mattered. I was allowed to cook frozen Totino's party pizzas and they let me help cook dinner. Jamie took me shopping for make-up and allowed me to babysit her son. I grew to be a stronger person, even though I was always up to no good. I would drink liquor out of their cabinet when they were not home. I also had a boy over and lost my virginity on their basement floor. I was caged my whole childhood and this was my first freedom, and I never wanted to go back home.

I really missed my dog Rambo and asked Jamie to sneak me over to my parents' house so I could see my dog over the fence - and she did. Dad was not allowed to see me or talk to me, but he would show up once in a while unexpectedly. He and mom would show up all dressed up and have new gold and diamonds on in their LeBaron convertible. They were still spending the lawsuit winnings they had hid from the cops and looking like they were having the time of their lives.

Dad bought me a gold chain and started kissing my ass the few times I saw him. I remember how odd it was, and then one day it all made sense...It was time for court. He begged me to change my police report.

He told me Charity and Chuck had already agreed to do it. This was the advice of his crooked lawyer to secretly convince the three of us to change our testimonials and redo police reports from that night. He begged me and so did Mom, making it impossible for me to say no. He told me he was going to go to jail forever if I didn't do it.

I was fifteen years old and Jamie took me downtown to a lawyer's office to change my statement. The story was that Charity and I made it all up because we were mad at Dad for kicking her and her fiancé out. I walked into the fancy oak office and sat down where the lawyer told me to. I remember feeling mad at him because I knew he was fixing all this for my dad. The lawyer slid a Bible out and told me to raise my left hand and put the right one on the Bible.

"Do you swear to tell the whole truth and nothing but the truth, so help you God?" I thought nothing of the Bible and said "Yes" as I nodded my head. I knew I was going to tell whatever lies this lawyer told me to tell. At this very second, my right hand was pierced in pain. The pain was so insane I pulled my hand off of the Bible and put it under the table to massage it with my left. It felt like a nail pierced straight through my hand. I thought for sure everyone in the room could see my pain. It was so severe I couldn't hide it from my face. It felt like a knife stabbed me right through the hand. After a few seconds the pain subsided and I said "yes" and "no" to whatever the lawyer told me to say "yes" and "no" to. I remember thinking he knew he was telling what lie to say without actually telling me to say it. I forgot all about my hand and never mentioned it to anyone.

Several weeks later, Mom and Dad showed up at Jamie's house to get me and take me back home. I wanted to live with my Aunt Jamie forever. I couldn't even hide my sadness and on the ride home I remember my father randomly saying, "I am a good dad, Danny. I raised you guys the best I can. I'm a good dad, right?" I answered the only safe response

– "yep" - and we went home. It was just the three of us and things were smooth and quiet. We would go out to visit Charity out in Mead, Nebraska, where she and Chuck lived together. I would spend a few weekends with her and pulling bong hits all day and night, doing coke and getting drunk. It was good times for this tenth grade girl.

Dad still had tons of money and was gambling it away as fast as possible. I was caught drinking in school and got kicked out for the year and sent to ICC, a school for bad kids. Mom and Dad would let me have boyfriends now and I was smoking pot with Dad every day. When Dad would lose his mind, I would stand up to him and, even though he still verbally abused Mom, he stopped hitting us for a while. The fear of jail seemed to linger over him now.

I barely graduated high school and wanted to go to Metro community college. Mom had pushed me to go and even took me to get signed up to go for law enforcement. That weekend before classes would start, Dad got me stoned and convinced me to not go to school on Monday and come to Wisconsin with him to see my Aunt Tamera. He convinced me that I didn't really need college to become a cop and I should just smoke weed and party all the way to Wisconsin with him. That's what we did from fifteen to eighteen years old - I smoked weed, dropped acid and did coke and meth with my dad and Uncle Timmy. I slept with a different boy and went to rock concerts every weekend. I spent those years doing drugs, having sex and playing pool at Big John's Billiards over off L St.

I was working at a hardware store and got caught stealing for a friend. This guy I had made out with when I was 13 now had a wife and a baby. She told me while checking out in my line that it was so hot in her home her baby was getting rashes. I told them to just go get a window air conditioner and I would let it go through my line for free. I had been doing it for the last few months for my dad and Uncle Timmy anyways; but I got caught the next week over the air conditioner because it was such a large item.

My father was so mad that I had gotten caught, plus I had to go to court because I was being charged with theft by deception. I remember Dad had convinced me I was for sure going to go to jail for a few years. I was so sad that I ate a whole box of twenty-four allergy pills and tried to kill myself. But I woke up the next day and just went on living. Those months were the worst months for me when I look back. Dad was yelling at me every day and no one in my home would talk to me.

I had two best friends from Pizza Hut where I started working - Tom and Cody. We would hang out together and Tom would convince me it was going to be OK and nothing bad was going to come of the court date. Cody shared a piece of advice with me I never forgot: "Suicide is a permanent solution to a temporary problem." I'm thankful for those two, even though I would end up hurting them as well. Tom and I even had matching tattoos. We shot pool all the time together and became very close.

The trial day finally came and I walked up to the judge with my parents. The judge gave me a fifty-dollar fine and sent me on my way. After months of my father telling everyone what a "fuck-up" I was and convincing me I was going to jail, all I received was a tiny fine. Dad took away my car and I lost my job.

During another fight between Mom and Dad, Mom came down and hid in my bedroom, which was now located in the basement on 39th and Harrison. At this time in my life, I was still working at Pizza Hut. Dad came downstairs to switch it up and fight with me. We got into a fist fight; he threw himself onto me and we fell to my bed. The bed collapsed under our combined weight. My dad took his thumbs and put them into my eye sockets, pushing down so hard I could feel my eyeballs were about to pop. They were pressed against the back of their sockets and I knew they were going to explode. I screamed for help from my mother or sister for the first time in my life, but no one came.

I grabbed my dad's favorite gold chain around hanging from his neck and yanked on it. Dad jumped up off me, fearful I would break his chain. I stood up and made my way to my phone. With shaky hands, I called my boss, Michelle, and asked her if I could move in with her and her roommates. She said, "Absolutely", and I walked out the front door. At this point, I didn't care if I lived or died anymore and it had been like that since I was fifteen years old. I remember I would drive my 1979 red Camaro through red lights, just hoping to get hit and be killed. I had a baseball bat in my car and a tire knocker ready to use on anyone who tempted me. I can remember chasing after cars in road rage and even jumping out with a bat and telling grown men to get out of their car. I would chase people down for miles trying to get them to get out of their car so I could beat them. I must have always looked just crazy enough for people to not get out.

I was a terrible roommate, getting drunk all the time. The first night I stayed with Michelle, the cops dropped me off and I walked in the door to puke in the bathroom. The guy I was dating proposed and I said yes because I didn't know how to say no. I was cheating on him and on every boy I ever dated. I would call them impulsively and then sleep with them, only to never answer their call again.

I couldn't shovel drugs into my body any faster. I was waitressing at the time and got pregnant. I immediately had an abortion, because I didn't even consider it was a baby in my belly, and that's what you did in my house when you got pregnant. Mom had had an abortion and so had my aunts. It was normal in my world, plus Dad had always told us if we ever got pregnant he would kick us down the stairs and we wouldn't be pregnant anymore. I was so wrong in the head about so many things.

I was lost and lonely and shoveling drugs down my throat as fast as possible. My Mom wasn't talking to me and neither was Charity, because Dad wasn't letting them. Charity and Dad were best friends again and I was not welcome to call Mom or visit. Charity had come over once where I was living when we threw a party. She pretended to drink and pretended to get drunk in front of my friends; I thought this was so weird. Why wouldn't you want to be drunk?

After about a year of not seeing Mom, I decided to stop by the house and just hug her. My newly acquired fiancé and I went to the door. My mom answered the door, but she acted so strangely and was almost scared we were there. I walked in through the house to find my sister and Dad hanging outside in the back yard with some guy I used to date. I knew instantly that's why they hadn't talked to me all this time. I found out Charity had liked him when I dated him, so when I moved out her and Mom put a note on his car.

I ended up becoming friends with my dad again and Mom was allowed to talk to me with his consent. I tucked my tail between my legs and moved back home sometime later. I didn't know where to go or what to do, but I didn't want to marry this boy and I just wanted to go home. I moved into the basement of our small home, living on an air mattress, with Charity and my old boyfriend living upstairs.

They all treated me badly and Dad yelled at me the first week I was home. I got a job roofing cedar shake for a local company. I had never been on a roof before, but when I opened up the Omaha World Herald I saw an ad for roofers needed and thought "how hard can it be"? So I went to the job site and forced the foreman to hire me. With a two-minute lesson, I was roofing the next day and I was making great money. Between paying Dad rent, the coke shoveled up my nose, and smoking the rest in meth, the money was gone. I was picking my body apart, because that is what meth addicts do. I was doing coke with the foreman and the whole crew. I shot myself in the leg with a roofing staple and started wreaking havoc on the crew. I was sleeping with one of them who was married, and disappeared for a few days. I was hanging out at strip clubs and just being the meanest person I could be. I was fired and moved on to work at the same slaughterhouse my dad had worked at. I never really looked on the outside like the monster I had become on the inside.

I worked with all these guys and was just about the only woman. I hung out at the bars with Braindead, Dog, Mario and Ese. Dog lost one of his testicles in a bar fight and when he pissed me off I would bring it up and he would get mad at me. I was threatening to kill grown men at twenty years old, what seemed like every day. I would pull the spinal cord from the dead cattle carcasses hanging from the racks, about a four-foot-long cord, and I would put it into my mouth; it would hang like long bloody tennis shoe strings and I would spit it out at the men who worked with me. Nope, no one ever messed with me and they called me "Loca weta", which was their way to call me "crazy white girl". I can honestly say that not one of the Mexicans I worked with ever once treated me badly. They actually seemed to care about me and that I was drunk all the time. They would try to talk to me to stop the direction I was going. I was never sexually discriminated or harassed in all the time I worked with hundreds of illegal and legal Mexicans. But I must say that we worked like dogs for our minimum wage in the slaughterhouse. Grown men would piss themselves because they couldn't get off the line for a piss break without getting in trouble.

My sister had found a good job working at Ameristar Casino over in Council Bluffs. Dad and she convinced me to go over there to get a job. I was working way too hard for way too long at the packing houses and I permanently injured my shoulder throwing meat into boxes. I would get off work to stop at the bar for a triple shot of Jim Beam then go home to fall asleep exhausted at the kitchen table. I was an alcoholic and a drug addict. The meth had become my breakfast, lunch and dinner.

CHAPTER 14: BOWLING AND BLOSSOMING LOVE

I decide to go ahead and apply for dealer school and was surprised I got in. Charity had pushed them to hire me for Dad's will and so now I had to get clean and sober. I got clean, but not sober. Getting clean was easy, because all my drug dealers were MIA at the time. One, who was my favorite Laos gang member, is said to be in prison for life in California. I knew the get clean kits were not one hundred percent foolproof, because I had used them in the past and they'd failed me. So I quit smoking pot and just stuck to drinking, and meth and coke when I could get my hands on it. I passed the piss test that was at the end of the 30-day dealer school, so I had 30 days to clean out my system and got my dealers license.

This was a huge financial and social step up for me. I had to shower and do my hair and make-up every day for work. I was good at working full-time and being on time thanks to working at the slaughterhouses. Working on an assembly line, the guys you work with need you to show up or they get stuck filling in the blanks for you. Without all the drugs eating my skin and brain cells, I started to see I may be smart and pretty, despite what I had been led to believe. I had always talked like a man; even my mannerisms were that of a man's. My conversations always seemed to flow like a lifelong buddy's when I would speak with strangers. Now, around twenty-one years old, working at the casino and adjusting to being friendly, I grew to love being there.

I would take Charity and Mom on shopping splurges and was spoiling Mom with all this new and easy money I was now making. I took her to the mall to get her hair cut regularly, and one day picked out a boy named Joe to color my own hair. I told Joe all my crazy stories to make him laugh. A few weeks later, I saw Joe at the casino while I was working. He was with a cute brunette boy about my own age. I said "Hi" to

Joe and then said "Hi" to Phil. I asked him, "So, you do the hair thing too?" He said, "No, I do the computer thing." I thought he was cute and I had never dated a nerd before.

I always dated a few boys at one time and usually had another one lined up. I never had any real girlfriends; all my friends were guys. If a guy really liked me, I would break up with them. If I really liked a guy and thought he didn't like me, I would break up with him. I would obsessively call or not ever call a boy, depending on my bipolar mood or how bored I was.

I loved going out to the clubs to go dancing and shooting pool at Big John's. I had gotten to be pretty good at it and would win most of the time. I dated a few boys and, being Valentine's Day weekend, I had two separate dates lined up so I wouldn't feel lonely. I was at work when I saw that Phil kid again, alone this time at the blackjack table. He was playing at one of the tables on the lower level when I noticed him; I was headed to take my break. I had seen him a few times in the last month and decided to go over and flirt with him. I stood in the center of the gaming pit and flipped my long, brown, Victoria's Secret hair from side to side. Nothing happened; he didn't even look up, so I tried again -this time shifting my hip and flipping my hair. Still, he didn't look up.

I headed over to the table he was playing at, and he slid out a hundred-dollar chip for a bet to play one hand. It is playfully argued to this day as to whether or not he played that hand to try and impress me. He lost and headed my way as I walked in his direction. I said, "So you spending Valentine's Day alone, too?" "Yeah", he replied. I said, "Why don't you, me, and Joe all go out to a club this Friday?" He said, "Sure, let's do that!" So I gave him my number and left the pit to go up for my break.

Later that night, I saw him as I passed by the roulette wheel and he stopped me and said, "Hey, what are you doing Thursday?" I said, "Nothing!" He suggested just the two of us go out that Thursday. I said,

"Sure." I knew what he was up to. He wanted to make it a date and I was fine with it. We chatted on the phone all night before our first date. He picked me up in a piece of crap beater, which I didn't mind. By this time, I had dated half of Omaha and knew what kind of car a guy had said nothing about their personalities.

I dated the wealthiest to the poorest boys in Omaha and almost always said yes if someone asked me out. I could size up a boy's personality very fast by their actions. Most guys I dated would go goofy over me; even parade me around to parties to show all their friends what they caught. I didn't mind - I played the parts they all needed played. I enjoyed dating men who were mean to girls. I could get them to think I was everything they ever wanted and then never call them again or even answer their phone calls. I would try to hurt boys who thought they were tough. Unfortunately, I hurt a lot of good guys too, guys who were innocent victims, along my destructive path. I left a long trail of hurt and confused boys who I can never apologize enough to. I had dated abusive guys who thought they could try these tactics with me. This would result in me kicking their dashboards apart and threatening to cut their pet's heads off. Even the most abusive men would run for the hills.

Phil picked me up for our first date and I suggested we go to Big John's Billiards to shoot pool, and he agreed. He was so cute and funny, even being playfully sarcastic. I was shooting triple shots of Jim Beam and kicking his butt in pool. I liked the way his veins popped out on his forearms over his muscles and he was proving to be smarter than most boys I had dated. He was witty and I didn't intimidate him with my very masculine personality.

We played pool for a bit then I said, "If I win this game, you have to kiss me." I won the game and we kissed for the first time - an hour after he picked me up. It was the worst kiss ever, but I didn't mind. He was still cute and fun to talk to. He told me his friend had died very recently. Within a week or so, his friend Jimbo was shot dead at a party and his cousin was in the hospital. I didn't take what he said too seriously at the time, because I usually wasn't interested in anything real anyone had going on in their lives. I had no hopes for this boy to make it longer than a week or two.

We finished up the pool game and walked out to the parking lot. We passionately made out the whole time and even on the drive all the way to my home. When we pulled into the drive I said, "You want to do something again tomorrow night?" He said, "Yeah, what do you want to do?" I replied, "We could just watch a movie or something. You gotta VCR, don't ya?" He said, "Yeah". So I said, "Let's just rent a movie." I had no intentions of watching a movie. The next day he picked me up and we had to go by the hospital to pick up his cousin Jay, who was also there visiting his brother Chad. Chad was in a recovery room, recovering from being shot. I stayed outside the room while Phil went in to say hi. He came out a few minutes later with Jay and we all left together and got into Phil's car.

Phil was in a bowling league on Friday nights, so I was stuck going bowling first. I thought only dorks bowled, but this guy Phil wasn't a dork - he was cool. Jay hopped in the back seat with Phil in the driver's seat and me riding shotgun. Jay looked down at his floor board and kicked a box at his feet. Jay said, "Phil, you went out and bought a VCR today?" I smiled and slowly turned to look at Phil, who also smiled and just kept driving while looking forward. I thought it was cute that he lied to me. It was an inside joke now.

So we got to the bowling alley and the three of us walked inside. Joe, our hair-dressing mutual friend started walking towards us and yelled, "Phil, you came in for a haircut and you got new clothes today?" Phil probably wanted to choke him. Whenever a boy had done something to impress me in the past, it was just that, something they were doing to impress me. Phil knew I was going to sleep with him and had no intentions of pointing out what he was doing to impress me. It was adorable. He didn't buy me flowers on the first date or try and show me how his dad is buying an island off the coast of blah blah. This was different and he was busted, but he played it cool.

That night we had a great time together. I playfully flirted with all his friends and flirted more with Phil. We went to his brother's house later and I stayed the night with him. I had to call my father at midnight, which was my curfew, and tell him I wasn't coming home for the first time ever. When he went to yell at me, I just hung up the phone on him. That morning it was odd to meet his brother and sister-in-law. The next day, Phil was going to meet my family. When we landed in the driveway on 39th Street I paused and looked over at Phil seated in the driver seat and said, "Promise me that when you meet my dad you won't do any money deals with him." He agreed. I can't recall anyone ever making through the lion's den without a scratch. So we walked into the house and the first thing Phil saw was a loaded handgun on the armrest of couch.

I explained, "It's nothing, don't worry about it. But it's loaded, so don't touch it." My family was in the backyard and we were headed out to them when I turned and said to him, "Welcome to the Adams Family, da da da dum", and then snapped my fingers twice in reference to the TV Series. With a heavy heart, I meant it. The first person Phil was to be introduced to was Charity, who randomly decided to give him a dirty look and walk away. Then Dad and Mom came in and we all talked for a few, and then Phil and I went downstairs. My bedroom was a bit of a den room with a large TV, a few end tables and my large salt-water aquarium. We sat down on my bed that kind of doubled as the couch.

Within a few minutes, Charity came right down and with a smile offered Phil some brownies. He wouldn't eat them until I tried a bite. He looked at me and said, "I had to be sure they weren't poisoned because your family is crazy." I remember being relieved that he saw it too. He actually saw right through the Dan Gardner song and dance that usually reeled everyone into Dad's persuasive ways. He saw my mom as this puppet victim of my father's. I couldn't believe it. At that moment I felt something else for him. We hung out a lot after that; I believe it was every single day. We were also always on the phone together.

One date night, we were walking into a restaurant for lunch and he said something as we crossed the parking lot. I don't remember what it was, but I didn't like it so I smacked him across the face. It was playful and not very hard, but I knew it hurt and I followed it with a smile and a laugh. Phil gently but firmly grabbed my hand and stopped to say, "Look, if we are going to do this, you can't be doing that. OK?" He said it with a nod of reassurance from me and a small smirk. I said, "OK". This was so strange to me because any other guy would have either been mad at me the rest of the night or would have thrown a temper tantrum because I hit them. No, this boy was no boy at all - this little bowling computer nerd was a real man. I recognized that I never knew what a man was before, but I noticed immediately that this is how a man should behave - and I loved it. He controlled his temper and would think of others before he would speak. That became my first definition of a real man and a real leader to me that day.

We went over to his brother's house, where his sister-in-law did in-home daycare; when we walked in the basement door all the kids were staring at us. He looked at these things staring owl-eyed at us from the ground and said, "Hey, what's going on, guys?" "What's everybody up to today?" These toddlers could hardly talk, they were barely just walking. Phil put on a little show with words and his funny charm and made them all laugh.

We went upstairs to see his niece, Mariah, and she ran into his arms and Phil said, "Hello, beautiful". It was at that moment I couldn't wait to hear him say those words to me. That was it - I was in love, head over heels in love, with a guy I had just met. I knew I was going to marry him! That's gotta sound crazy to you, and it was crazy to me, but this boy named Phil was everything I never knew I always wanted and I was going to be with him forever.

We spent every moment together. Despite working opposite shifts at our jobs, we made our relationship work. It took Phil a while to see we were in this long-term. I remember that first week I told him I loved him and laughed about it. I remember telling him he would be saying it back soon enough and that we were going to be together forever. He looked at me as if I were absolutely crazy. But I was sure of it. "I bet you tell me you love me within a week," I proclaimed. Sure enough, that week we went to a movie together, and like always I enjoyed pointing out the flaws in the movie. We were watching a Mel Gibson movie and gas was pouring from a car - but as it poured out it was pouring out uphill. I leaned over to whisper, "I don't think gasoline can pour out a vehicle uphill." Phil leaned in and said, "And that is why I love you." It naturally and accidentally flowed out of his mouth and I screamed and hit his shoulder saying, "I told you, I told you would say it!"

Phil later confessed that he had told his coworker, "This is going to be a wild ride, and I am just going to hold on for as long as it will last!" We had a couple of large arguments, but never broke up or even went to bed fighting. Phil was wise with his words and I only knew how to scream and break my own things. He was smarter than me and would rewind the day to get to where I first got upset. I always came out feeling foolish for the little nothings that I would let escalate, and felt even more foolish cleaning up my own stuff I broke when I would get mad.

Phil moved in with his friend Joe and Cousin Jason, and I pretty much spent every night there too. We would spend a lot of time hanging out with my parents and going fishing with them. Phil and my dad hit it off, and my dad was regularly calling Phil, "Son." My dad just loved Phil. They hung out every weekend and became close friends. Being around Phil, my father behaved better. It made my dad too embarrassed to act the way he would normally act because he, too, could see Phil was no fool. Dad was just a better person around Phil.

When it came time to renew his lease with his friends at the apartment, my dad and I convinced Phil to just move in with me. So for the next year or two we lived in my parent's basement together. These were good days and, for once, everyone was getting along.

CHAPTER 15: CONVERSION AND CONVERSATIONS

Some of you can probably relate to my childhood, while others are blown away with all the craziness of it all. By the time I had met Phil, I had been a proud atheist for a few years. I hated any God, even if there was one. God had never shown up in my childhood eyes to kill my dad like I had prayed for and neither did the Devil.

When Phil and I first started dating, he would tell me short stories from the Bible. I had tons of questions, all of which were to try and make him see there really was no God. I was positive at twenty-two years old that Santa Claus, the Easter Bunny and God were just the same type of lies fed to us as tradition to be good and behave. When I caught my mom lying to me in first grade about the Easter Bunny that she had promised me was real, it helped throw the possibility about God being real as well right out the window. I believed I put the Easter Bunny in the same category as church or God. Mom did say prayers from time to time, but they were just a quick thing we did at night as kids.

One night Phil and I were laying there in bed, and Phil told me that the Bible said there was only one way into heaven. I trusted Phil at this point and asked him, "Well, what is it?" I was fairly certain it was doing good deeds, going to church and saying the rosary regularly, plus eating that white thing the priest feeds you. He said, "Nope, it is simply believing and receiving Jesus. I said, "What? What are you talking about?" Phil said, "The Bible says that if any man calls upon the name of the Lord, and confesses with his mouth that Jesus is their Lord and savior, you are welcomed into God's kingdom." I thought this was a bit ridiculous, but wanted to hear more. "So you mean all the bad stuff I did doesn't matter?" Phil said, "Nope. You just pray to God and confess you have sinned and that you turn from your sin now, and accept the fact that Jesus died on the cross for your sins so that whoever believes in this and confesses it with their mouth is a saved child of God and will be welcomed into heaven when they die." "So wait, does this mean I have to never drink again or curse or what?" He said that it's not like that; you are telling God you are now His, and acknowledging Jesus' sacrifice on the cross.

We talked about it for hours. I had many questions, and luckily Phil knew the Bible inside and out, so all his answers were lined up with it. I couldn't ask him a question he couldn't answer. I was impressed. This kid really knew what he was talking about. "But what about you?", I asked. You do drugs with me, we have sex and we ain't married. Ain't that sinning? He said, "Yes". I said, "Well, don't that mean we are not going to heaven when we die?" He said, "No. According to the Bible, once you are saved, you are always saved. So I asked, "Well, what if I go kill someone tomorrow?" He said, "Well you are going to heaven, but I would probably question whether you said the prayer with your heart or if you said it as a joke. You see, once you're saved, Jesus comes into your heart and starts to change the things you want to do."

Later, Phil went home and I lay there in bed thinking over all we had talked about. My bedroom was in the basement and Mom and Dad were living upstairs with Mark and Charity at the time. I stared at the ceiling for a while and then went for it. I told God about the sins I had known were sins and told him how I felt about them. At this time, I had had two abortions and was so mean to people. I had lied and stolen my entire life. I had hurt so many people and slept with so many men I couldn't count. I cried and told God I was sorry. I told God I turn from it and accept that Jesus died on the cross for my sins as my only passage into heaven. Nothing happened. I didn't feel anything. Lightning didn't strike the house and no angel appeared. For me, nothing happened. I did feel like at least I covered my base with God.

The next morning over coffee, I shared what happened with everyone. No one in my house knew what the Bible said you needed to do to go to heaven. Even Dad was surprised about it, and he was an altar boy for at least a year growing up. Phil shared it all with them when they would have questions, because we all had a few. My Dad absolutely loved everything about Phil, always. Dad could never act crazy in front of Phil for some reason. Dad seemed to truly respect Phil's opinion of him. The two of them would sit around the kitchen table talking and doing bong hits for hours. I worked nights at the casino, so Phil would hang out with dad after he got off work and wait for me to come home. Dad called Phil "Son" all the time, as soon as we started dating. Phil and Dad spent years fishing together over at the creek and down on Bass Lake. Phil's friends would come over and Dad would entertain them like he always did. They all loved him even though some wouldn't be allowed back by their wives. Their relationship was special. Dad really seemed to love Phil and the house was safe with Phil around. Phil was calm-minded and even-tempered; Dad just loved having him around.

I told my friends at the casino what I had done. No one knew what I was talking about. I asked everyone and encouraged them to do it too - to pray and accept Jesus! I was surprised one day in the break room when a close friend, Jim, who was about sixty years old, said he believed in God, but didn't want to do "all that." This was the response I got from most people. They believed in the Bible, but weren't going to do it. To me that was like saying you have cancer and you have the medication but "you ain't going to do all that." Through those years, I maybe told fifty people when the conversation would pop up about God and His son Jesus.

CHAPTER 16: TANTRUMS AND TOBACCO

Dad was still crazy as always, but he would grow softer through the years and less violent. Phil had immediately become the son Dad never had. The two of them became inseparable, going fishing down at the Base Lake and spending every night together while waiting for me to get off of work. Dad begged, pleaded and convinced us to buy the home he lived in because they were going to lose it due to their gambling debts; so, with much hesitation, we bought it so they wouldn't lose it.

Unfortunately, Dad caused a huge rift between Charity and me because he had also asked her to help him out and begged her to buy his home. He was supposed to tell her that the plan had changed, but she found out the wrong way and swore we betrayed her and wanted to never talk to any of us ever again. She had been looking at houses to buy for all four of them to live together. Dad did things the shady Dan Gardner way and her feelings were hurt. Looking back, I should have just told her what he was doing - but I didn't want anybody upset. A few months after we had bought Mom and Dad's home, Phil and I moved into a house out in west Omaha with an in-law apartment for my mom and dad and we rented out their old home. Charity eventually forgave us for not telling her right from the start and was back in our lives within a year.

Phil and I were married down at the courthouse one day in Omaha. I didn't want a wedding and really had no one to invite from my side of the family, so we spent two weeks on our honeymoon instead. We went on our honeymoon to Mexico and it wasn't soon after that we were pregnant with our first child. We had a baby boy we named Angelo. The delivery was complicated because the epidural did not take, and after 4 hours of pushing they rushed me to the operating room to perform a C-section. They were rushing, because they waited too long and gave me a local anesthetic and begin cutting my stomach open. I could feel the excruciating pain of every inch they were cutting, including their hands inside my stomach pulling him out. They had to physically hold me down. The anesthesiologist was standing by with needle in hand, waiting for the cord to be cut. As soon as they cut the cord, he hit me the drug and I drifted off within seconds. I fell in love with my son from the second he was conceived and Phil and I would spend every second we had playing with him.

Dad, while living in our basement, would have moments where he would get mad and not talk to us. He still kept a loaded gun in his apartment and I would still have to get involved when he would yell and threaten Mom. Their apartment was not connected to our house by a door, but the walls were thin. If the argument sounded bad, I would go downstairs and sit on my dryer to listen for a bit to make sure he wasn't going to hit her. I could tell by listening in on his rant what type of argument it was. Fortunately for us all, when they lived with us I had gotten the upper hand on Dad because now that he was under my roof I could kick him out and keep Mom. I know he was aware of that and I also know he knew that I knew this. So even though it was never discussed, he now had a cap on his temper level or would suffer the consequences.

Dad never let go and still had full control over my mother and sister. They made no decision in life without running it past his twisted, self-centered mind. He had his hands buried in Charity's pockets. Her and her husband's relationship hung on a pendulum that Dad kept on his finger, swinging it in any direction that would make him money like getting some of her husband's 401K and savings. Dad did this with so many couples through the years that it's impossible to tell them all to you. Mostly it was our family that was the victim of Dad's horrible meddling and poisonous interventions. Dad would convince one to break it off with the other and also give him all their gold, diamonds, guns etc.

that was worth anything. Unfortunately, Charity loved Dad so much that she allowed him to use her often.

One of the last major arguments I had gotten into with my father was over him attempting to destroy Charity's marriage. I caught him on the phone talking bad about her husband in horrible ways that were not true, and convincing her to take all his money and take the kids. I even recall him guaranteeing her she would end up with full custody if she mentioned to the courts he molested the kids. I screamed at him one afternoon over his meddling, while he sat on the couch in my house. He knew what he was doing was wrong. He actually said something like, "Fine, I'll never talk about that stuff with Charity again." But he was lying. I was holding him accountable for everything he was doing to her and he was willing to admit it just to sneak out of the argument.

He loved her husband, Mark, but for his own financial gain pointed out flaws in him that Charity never even saw or cared about. Dad spent years making fun of Charity's husband behind his back, causing them to fight. He mocked and made fun of Mark in every single conversation Charity and he ever had. There was no way she could see who her husband was anymore. Dad had excluded all his family from his life and Charity had always only known one way - to look for any reason to fight and then cut the person out of her life to punish them. She was always screaming at me, or my mom or her husband. It was just too much. It was always hard living up to her random expectations that seemed to change minute to minute; I walked on eggshells trying not to break them my entire life with her and my father. But the truth is they liked it when they broke and constantly changed the steps, which made it impossible to satisfy them. They both had a hard time with peace and confrontation felt more normal.

I had opened a tobacco shop because, even though I didn't smoke at the time, I was desperate to quit being a dealer while pregnant at the casino.

People would say the worst things to me: "Oh, you're pregnant? Well, get ready for 18 years of hell." So I opened Danny's Tobacco Shop on 114th and Dodge. It slowly turned into a pipe shop because the cigarettes were not selling. I enjoyed owning the store and was able to have my son with me. Mom and Dad would come in and work the store for me. I always found it funny to catch my Dad telling people it was his store, or that he gave us the money to buy the store. I also didn't mind that he was stealing from me. The store made enough profit that when he stole his cigarettes and made deals on the side it didn't affect our profits enough to cause an argument.

I was pregnant just weeks after Angelo was born with my daughter Domiano. I was nervous having a girl, because I had no idea what to expect. She was so precious and I knew she was going to be my best friend. Her delivery went so differently than Angelo's. It was a scheduled C section with no complications.

Dad and I were getting along. He loved to go to garage sales out in the 'rich people neighborhoods' with me. Phil had even set them up with a computer and taught them how to sell stuff on eBay for profit. Dad was a garage sale, eBay-selling maniac. He would shoot his jalapeno green truck into people's driveways in the middle of their sale and jump out looking for anything he could make a few hundred bucks off of. I loved seeing him get so excited to find a saxophone for twenty-five dollars that he knew was worth three hundred dollars on eBay.

Mom would work the store for that next year and Dad and I would hit garage sales together. It was the best moments we ever had as a father and daughter. I would talk to him about the way he treated Mom and Charity and he would get upset with me saying, "There you go again, trying to teach me a lesson and tell me how to live my fucking life."

Once, Dad and I were out garage sailing in this very wealthy ranch community; every house had a horse and a personalized driveway with their names carved in the entry archways. I was nine months pregnant with Domiano and wasn't paying attention to my driving, so I hit a mailbox. This wasn't just any mailbox; it was a huge handcrafted replica of the property. I smashed it and Dad started freaking out yelling at me, "Go! Go! Before anyone sees you." At that second, I kept going, but when I pulled into the next driveway to turn around, Dad was even more upset. "I can't fucking believe you're turning around. That mailbox is gonna cost you five hundred dollars. What you're doing makes no fucking sense."

I pulled into the driveway and got out of our 1999 Jeep Cherokee. Dad sat silent and disappointed in me. A woman in her pajama robe came casually out to greet me. I started telling her how sorry I was and that I would gladly pay for another one. She laughed and said, "Don't be silly, darling. My son made this one and he can build me another." I was so relieved because that mailbox was insane with detail. I couldn't thank the lady enough. When I got back in the car, Dad started telling me how lucky I was, and that Phil was going to be pissed that I wrecked his Cherokee. I called Phil immediately, because I was a little shaken up. "Hey baby, I just wanted to tell you I just hit a huge mailbox." "Are you alright?" Phil said softly. I said, "Yes". He said, "Is your dad with you?" "Yep," I giggled. He made a sigh and said, "How's that going?" I said, "Eh, you know," Then Phil chuckled and said, "Well, I'm glad you're OK. I love you, but I gotta take this call, Bye, babe." "Well, what did he say?" Dad asked excitedly. He wanted to hear that Phil was pissed off at me. I said, "About the Cherokee?" Dad said, "Yeah." I said softly to my father, "Dad, Phil didn't even ask about the Cherokee, because he doesn't care about the Cherokee. Dad, Phil asked me if I was OK. You see, Dad, these things happen, and will always happen, but when they happen to you, you freak out about it - like not too long ago with your truck."

A few months prior to that day, Dad was driving his beloved jalapeno green Ford when a rock bounced out of a work truck in front of us and hit Dad's truck. Dad lost his mind down the interstate, with me sitting in the passenger seat. He could have killed us chasing that work truck down to force the guy to pull over, so Dad could check his own truck for damage. There was no damage, but I'm not kidding when I say he was weaving in and out of traffic like a ragged panicked person at extreme speeds. I looked down at my bulging belly and couldn't believe I had put my unborn child in this danger and swore this would never happen again. I told Dad what he had done and he would never drive with me in the car again.

I reminded him in the kindest way possible of how he put objects before his family. It made him mad and he would mumble something about me trying to teach him a lesson in life again. I never stopped trying to show my father a better way - a way with no drama and peace - but he always rejected it because he enjoyed his twisted ways. I never stopped trying to show him that there was a better way to live.

CHAPTER 17: A PARTY AND A PASSING

We all have those moments in our history that define our lives and how we became who we are today. We also have the moments that changed our hearts forever. Phil and I had both babies, and both were still in diapers, when we unlocked our store at 6:30am. I had just started to remove my daughter from her car seat when the store phone started to ring. This was an odd time for the phone to ring so I followed Phil to the front counter and watched as he answered the phone. He put his right hand slowly up to his mouth and lowered his head. I knew instantly, but asked to be sure. "Is it Dad, Phil?" "Is my Dad dead, Phil?"

Phil's eyes caught mine, and with tears forming he nodded his head softly. Mom was home alone with Dad so we locked up the store and headed that way. We dropped our kids off with Phil's sister-in-law and headed home to be with Mom. I had a party at the house the night before, with just close friends and family and all the children running around like crazy clowns. My party for the adults kind of sucked - it wasn't very fun - so I called Dad downstairs and said, "Dad, my party sucks. Will you get up here and liven things up?" In seconds, my Dad and Mom were out and up the back stairs. Dad walked in yelling at everyone and instantly everyone woke up. We laughed as Dad told all his old jokes and all his crazy stories. We laughed about the time he popped a wheelie up the street and fell off as Mom and the Harley kept going, with her sitting passenger up the street. He would point out your funny or sensitive flaws and everyone would laugh. He would have the whole room tearing up in laughter in seconds, putting on the one and only Dan show.

My friend Drew and I were about to have a girly shot called a Candy Apple Chocolate-covered Cherry, and I made one for Dad. Dad said, "I can't drink that shit, I'll have a fucking heart attack." Drew and I laughed and Dad had one shot. Later when the night started to wind down, Dad played with Angelo (who was about 1-1/2 years old), then we all sat down for a Texas Hold'em poker tournament. I looked at Dad across the table and thought about how terrible he looked. He was pale and yellow in color, and his eyes were darkened with tired circles around them. Dad quit going to the doctors and smoked two packs of Pall Mall non-filters a day.

But he looked different tonight and I thought to myself, "Dad looks like he is going to die soon. What a good time for him to die; we are getting along better than ever," I told myself. "He is really happy and had a great night doing what he loved best." Charity was coming into town; he had been complaining about her driving him nuts for days and laughed about how he would have to talk bad about me to keep her happy, so I remember thinking it would be best for Charity if Dad wasn't there to try and meddle in her marriage. He said goodnight to all of us at the party, who were people he had hung out with for years now, and went off to bed with Mom.

I walked in the front door to my parent's apartment and I saw Dad lying on the couch where he always lay. Mom was sitting on the floor with her face at his feet, holding them and crying. She was taking his feet and pounding them into her forehead weeping, and saying, "No, Danny, No, no, no!". It didn't seem real. She went to bed every night hoping he would be dead the next morning. I had also dreamed of this moment my entire childhood and prayed for it still for my mother's sake when Dad would still yell at her over nothing. He would still pick her dog up and hold a knife to the little Yorkie's throat and threaten to cut his head off. Yet here we were, crying.

Looking at him there with one eye open and the other half shut, his grin looked like a final wince of chest pain; I knew he had died of a heart attack watching TV while sitting on the couch. Phil and I hugged my mom; I cried in disbelief and I cried for my mom. When Mom went to the bathroom to get more tissue, I stuck my fingers to my dad's eyelids to force them shut. It was hard because he had been dead for hours and his sockets were bone dry. I wiggled and wiggled and finally got them to close, well mostly closed.

I couldn't believe he was never going to speak again. He was never going to yell at us or harm anyone ever again. As much as I loved him, I was glad he was finally dead. How could I love him so much, and had spent a few years even wanting to be just like him, but feel a sense of excitement that he was dead? Later, when things calmed down, I looked at Dad's forearm where Charity's two children's names were tattooed on. I remember Dad always calling me a "cheap bitch" because I refused to pay for him to get a tattoo of my two children's names as well. I got up and found a permanent marker and with great joy and a smile in my heart wrote "Angelo," and beneath that, "Domiano". I could hear my Dad's voice saying, "You cheap fucking bitch, you ghetto cheap fucking bitch." The thought of him mad at me one last time made me smile in a good way. Dad would have laughed about it as he yelled at me.

So many times, I tried to show my dad how his behavior affected us, especially harming my mom and Charity. My mother has told me more than once, "You know Danny, that's what your father always hated about you; you were always trying to teach him something." I'm assuming my mom has no idea how bad that hurts to hear from her. I am very content with having tried to always show my father a better way and that he hurt people with his words. I try to explain to her that this is why I know he loved me. He told me all the time that I was the thorn in his side. I like to think my father was forced to think about his behavior on several occasions because of me.

Charity was informed of Dad's passing by Mark, and they headed up to Omaha immediately. I remember Charity walking in the door and knew it was going to be very dramatic. We hadn't called the police yet to report Dad's death, because we knew Charity would want to see Dad one last time. She howled and wailed and fell to her knees at the couch next to Dad. She started to dry heave vomit, so we put Dad's large ashtray under her mouth in case she did actually vomit. Charity was devastated. When Dad was talking to her, the two of them would be on the phone every day. They were two peas in a pod. I was sure she was going to feel very empty now that her only friend was gone.

Charity, Mom and I are all my dad's victims; a prisoner to our own minds that are still controlled from the grave by our father 10 years later. When I think about Charity and Mom, I still get mad at Dad. This is his mess that he made, and that he left behind.

CHAPTER 18: CAGE FIGHTING AND CHANGES

Years flew by, and Phil and I were living in a beautiful split-entry home that sat on the corner of 156th and M. St. This is the home Dad had passed away in. After Dad died and Charity had gone away, I grew very bold. I was doing all types of things I would never do before. I would always face their nasty comments when I would try new things, but now no one was there to mock or ridicule me. I started doing whatever my heart wanted to do. I did art projects and house projects, like putting in a tile floor in my kitchen that I designed and laid myself. I started modeling for all kinds of stuff in Omaha, including a local video game, and a Nebraska Furniture Mart commercial that played during the Super Bowl in the Midwest. I even played an actress who died in a local horror film. I flew out to L.A. a couple of times for different things. We also shot a commercial as a family. I had sold the smoke shop to a young man named Harry and was just free to do everything I had ever wanted to do. Life was so good, and our two children Angelo and Domiano were just perfect kids.

Phil and I worked as a team parenting. I trusted Phil's judgment on how to raise them, mostly because I had never been around other kids growing up. Phil was one of six and his mom Donna always did daycare. Phil and I decided long before they were born that we would never lie to our kids and they would always see us as one team. We would never undermine each other in front of anyone, let alone our children. We tried to be consistent; 'no' meant 'no' in our home and we disciplined them right out of the gate. Our lives seemed just perfect. I really mean that. Phil and I were having a blast being parents. I was more of a hippie mom, letting the kids do all kinds of crazy things, like blow bubbles in the house and paint their bodies with permanent markers.

I loved being a stay-at-home mom. We played all day every day. We would bomb Dad with water balloons when he would pull in the driveway; me on the roof and the kids hiding behind bushes. I was always making something for us to play with or do.

Mom was doing great, too. As soon as Dad died, I called her father, George, who I had never spoken to. I said, "George, this is Danny - your granddaughter." He was so shocked. "Hi, Danny," he said. "I called to tell you my father is dead." He told me he had heard that. I said, "I want you to know your daughter Krissy is back. I want you to know she was a victim of his abuse until the day he died, and she is your seventeen-year-old little girl again who Dad took away from you. I want you to know she is not the monster he was and she misses you." My Grandpa, who I never knew, cried on the phone. He would become a father again to my mother and she would spoil him and spend hours at his feet holding his hand. They would fall in love all over again and she would be at his bedside as he slowly passed away. Mom would go on to rekindle her relationships with all her brothers and sisters, even little Jamie.

These times were the best times for us. Mom was free and so was I. Phil and I even joined a gym, Mid America Martial Arts in Omaha. We had gotten into watching MMA cage fighting, because Phil always loved the sport and wanted to try it, but never did. We would go down to South Omaha to watch boys fight In Tim Bazer's Omaha Fight Club. This kid named Drew Dober was our favorite and I asked him where he trained, and he said Mid America Martial Arts - so that's where we went. I was the only girl at first and that is just how I liked it. We were trained in Muay Thai by Kurt Podany and in Jujitsu by Ed and Aaron Cerrone. It was awesome. Phil and I would both eventually fight in a MMA bout one night at the Omaha Fight Club. Phil was the first fight of the night and he won the decision.

I was the main event and won by TKO in the second round. I even won the first Female MMA Fighter of the Year Award from Mid America. We would go out to the fights at least once a month. My best friend, Chessa (who also became a fighter), and I would dress in the sexiest outfits for fight night and were friends with everyone at the events, even the ring announcer. Drew Dober would later sign and fight for the UFC. Our fight family became a second family to us.

We made it to church once in a while, but I knew if we went out late on Saturday I wouldn't get stuck going to church on Sunday. So I tried to secretly make our Saturday nights late. Our summers were filled with fishing and camping with our Pontoon. Life was a great big party. I had parties at the house where all the kids would have a dance contest under my disco ball. It was so much fun. But even with all that, being almost famous, being in love with my husband, having the best kids and the best life I could ever imagine, life still was missing something. I always just wanted a little more - just to get on a billboard, just to get in a feature film, just one more pair of expensive boots, just more. I never felt content, always hunting for the next thing. Looking back, after I had met Phil, I had stopped stealing and lying. I guess I simply figured that I had met a good man and it changed me naturally. I didn't connect it to asking Jesus into my heart, several years before.

CHAPTER 19: RAIN AND RESEARCH

One day in our perfect little bubble we lived in, I was cleaning the house making my way into the front living room. As I looked down on the coffee table, I saw a book with a title that read something like "The Hebrew Translation of the Words of the Bible." This was strange. Phil's mom through the years would send me random 'God books', like "How to be a Woman of God" and stuff like that. I never read one and they would end up in a drawer. I didn't like that she would send me God books. I thought it was weird. I knew I didn't want to be a goofy Bible person like I saw his family as - all church, all God, all the time. I remember looking at the book as I cleaned the coffee table and thinking, "Oh great, is he going to tell me he wants to go to church more?", because I hated going to church. Yeah, it was a nice message and everything but I hated the music and I never liked how everyone looked like they were ready to drink the Kool-Aid. The people seemed phony and judgmental. We were going to a, "rich people church," as I liked to call them; it seemed like the right description.

Back then, I didn't think Phil's parents liked me and neither did any of his brothers and sisters. I remember when we were dating and living together, his family had one of his ex-girlfriends who was a "Good God Girl" pick him up from the airport when he went out to visit them. They were just hoping to get him away from me. His dad, when I told him one evening over the dinner table, without Phil around, that I was saved, he told me I wasn't. He told me how Phil's sisters were unhappy, that we were living together in Omaha. I cried and told Phil, and made him promise not to start a confrontation. Looking back I realize they only wanted what was best for Phil, but at the time I felt judged and rejected. So even after I was saved I didn't like the group that "being saved" would associate me with.

I knew Phil would tell me about this new book soon enough and I just brushed it off as nothing much. I knew he would cover it with me eventually. Phil and I truly are best friends, and we established a rule in the beginning of our relationship to never lie to each other. This took a few "Truth Sessions", but has been one of the foundational strengths of our relationship. Since we didn't lie to each other or keep a secret from each other, we knew everything we could possibly know about one another and I knew he would tell me what's up, so I never asked.

A few days went by and Phil and I were lying in bed together. Long after we had already kissed goodnight, I was still wide awake. I lay there listening to this loud, pounding rain forever. It usually takes me a good thirty minutes to fall asleep, but not Phil. That guy can fall asleep in under 60 seconds; it's the truth, and it makes me mad! He told me once he had learned a trick to falling asleep, just by imagining a book. He then opens the book, imagines the first page and stares at it until all the lines of writing disappears. Then he starts to turn blank pages until he falls asleep. This doesn't happen in my world. My brain starts to color those pages and turn it into a full library of flying books trying to escape the library, but lucky for me I have a shotgun and shoot the books down so they don't escape. Seriously, I think he has gotten so good at it that he just sees the book and starts snoring. So I lay there wide-eyed with no one to talk to. Our master bath has a skylight so you can imagine how loud sheets of rain can be.

That night, it was the loudest rain I had ever heard in my life. It sounded like I was in a steel shack the way the deafening sound filled the whole house. Then, without warning, the rain just stopped. It went from the loudest downpour one second to absolute silence the next. I thought, "Wow that was crazy!" I pictured our house driving down the road in a rainstorm, like a car and going under an overpass or bridge, because that's what it sounded like. Then I pictured a giant umbrella opening over the whole city of Omaha and stopping the rain.

Then, without warning: "PSHHHHHHH"; just like that the rain
came back. It was as just as loud and pounding as it was when it disappeared. "Absolutely nutty", I thought to myself. I was upset Phil didn't
get to hear that. I lay there and pictured our house coming out from
the protection of the overpass. Then, in my tired mind, I also saw the
umbrella collapse all the rain right onto our house. I couldn't believe
what I had just heard. In my thirty-two years, I had seen and heard all
types of neat rainstorms; but this took the cake. My last thought before
I drifted off to sleep was, "As soon as I wake up tomorrow, I'm going to
tell Phil about that crazy rain."

Tomorrow morning came and I had long forgotten about that crazy
rain storm. I was up and off with my two wonderful kids, and Phil was
off to work. Several days went by and Phil and I ended up together
alone in our car. I can't remember where we were going, but my mom
had stayed home with the kids. We were headed out to a town just outside of Omaha to do something and come right back. Phil was driving
and I was chewing his ear like normal. We were both feeling odd, because the kids weren't with us; we loved spending time with them and
never felt like we needed a "Kid Break". Matter of fact, we didn't want
to be away from them. Phil had both hands on the wheel and I was
looking right at him when he said, "I have something to tell you." My
heart sank immediately into my chest. Phil and I never have anything
we ever need to say seriously. We are two best friends who do everything together and had been through ten wonderful years together. I
instantly thought about money. I automatically thought I messed up
our account somehow and our money was off. "What is it?" I said in
an unfamiliar panic. "Do you remember the other night?" he said. The
words were relief to my ears. I sighed out loud and said (almost yelling)
joyfully, "The rain! Is that it? Oh my, you heard it too? I was going to
tell you about it and I completely forgot it even happened. I thought
you were going to say something serious. Wasn't it the nuttiest rain you
ever heard? I thought you were sleeping. It just shut off and then twen-

ty seconds later ... "BAM!" It came right back. Are you telling me you heard it too?"

My best friend stared straight ahead down the road and slowly started to shake his head and said, "No". He gently looked at me and whispered, "Are you telling me you heard it to?" Phil looked physically pale and sick. He was holding in tears. I sat back into my seat because I knew what he was about to say was going to be serious. "Phil, what happened? Phil, tell me what happened." This was uncharted territory for our relationship. We had been through serious situations many times in our adult lives that we faced together, but this was different.

Phil said, "I thought I dreamt it all, I thought I dreamt the whole thing. Are you serious you heard it? "Did you hear the rain shut off and turn back on again?" He was still speaking softly and slowly. "Yes", I said. "Now tell me what happened." "I was lying in bed next to you praying," Phil said, as tears flowed down his cheeks. It was the first time I had ever seen him cry. This is the same man who broke his hand training and didn't tell me for days because ... why cry about it? "I was lying in bed praying and I asked God that if He is truly God and the God of the universe, the God of the Bible (and I had been asking Him just to show me the truth and I would listen), that it would be absolutely nothing for Him to shut the rain off. And the rain shut off! So I lay there and decided that it didn't really just happen. I said to myself, "Fine, that could have just been a crazy coincidence." God, if that's truly you and you're the God of miracles from the Bible, then it would be nothing for you to turn that rain right back on. Pshhhhhhh! The rain slammed back down on the house in full force. I can't believe you heard it, too," he said. "I lay there frozen but trembling, tears running down my face. It felt like a horse kicked me in the chest, and it hurt so badly. I begged God for forgiveness, I received my answer and it was terrifying! I said, "I will never question you again."

(Phil) *Then the next morning, when I woke up I was still mentally overwhelmed over what happened. I had to be logical; I had to make some sense out of this. I decided it was more reasonable to me that I dreamt it all up, than the creator of Heaven and Earth would ever bother answering any of us, especially me. I looked around and walked over to the couch and sat down with my coffee. I decided for sure it didn't happen; it was all very real, but just a crazy dream. I picked back up where I left off with reading through the Bible, which was about one of Israel's judges named Gideon. The story of Gideon and the fleece is where God had an angel tell Gideon that he was to help free Israel from slavery, but Gideon wanted proof that he was sent from God. He asked for several signs, before he was ready to assemble the army to fight against their masters. One of the signs was putting a sheep's skin out on the ground overnight, and asking God to keep the fleece dry when the dew came and made the entire ground wet in the morning.*

God performed this for Gideon, but Gideon still was not satisfied and asked God for yet another sign the next night. This time he wanted God to make the dew only appear on the sheep's skin and have the entire ground around it to remain dry. God performed this sign for him as well. Once again, it was like a horse kicking me in the chest, and I had a hard time catching my breath. I began to cry again. What's going on? This doesn't make any sense! I'd always denounced any "God spoke to me" stories that I'd ever heard. I knew that the person was drinking or high if they ever thought God would reach out to them in a crazy way like this. Growing up, I always interpreted from church that the last written book of the Bible was the last time God ever would reach out to us until Jesus comes back, and even if He did it sure wouldn't be for someone like me. I had every opportunity to listen to and follow God, and most of my life I chose to feed the flesh and ignore God at every turn. I mean I really believed that so much that I derailed as many of these crazies as I could. I would use arguments; I was taught in church and Bible school, would use scripture, logic, reason, anything I could to help these "misguided" people get back on the right track. Could I have been wrong? Does God actually "answer" when we ask? Does He open when we knock? Do we find when we seek? I felt overwhelmed with God's presence, and asked God once again for forgiveness.

A few days have passed and all I can think about is what has happened. Why would He bother with me? I've tried to put some human logic on this, and each time I've had to stretch a little further. The best I could come up with was that this must be a crazy reality dream, caused by my memory of hearing the Bible stories before and somewhere, subconsciously, I knew the story of Gideon was coming up the next day, which caused it all. Everything in me screams how wrong this is, but every day I try to say it and convince myself that this is what happened. But something strange happened; every day that went by I don't feel better, I feel worse. I had to figure some other way to get this out of my head. I've never felt so conflicted before.

After a week or so, all I can think about every day, all day is "Why would you waste your time on me?" I wanted to get this out of my head; I needed to convince myself I'm crazy. I knew what I needed was someone to back me up! I need someone who is a no-nonsense, will speak their mind, will tell you you're being crazy and isn't afraid to slap someone to help them see the light - and I knew just the person, my best friend, and my wife. We always tell each other the truth, no secrets. Danny was the right person for the job. After I told Danny, I stopped questioning, and begin to pray and tell God whatever it was that He wanted me to do I would do, wherever He wanted me to go, I'd go. This was one of the hardest prayers to get out of my mouth, but was a pivotal point in my life."

As you can imagine, we were both a bit freaked out and decided not to tell anyone. Phil had told me he felt embarrassed and ashamed for doubting God and challenging Him like that. Phil was born and raised strict Baptist-style. His sisters, as children, didn't wear pants - only long dresses past the knees, and his mom wouldn't use wine for cooking.

They were very strict, but Phil was always searching for the truth. He once said, "There are people in other countries strapping bombs to their chest and blowing themselves up over their beliefs and their God. Who's to say their God is not the real God of the universe? I would never kill someone for my belief in God, so who's to say my God of the Bible is the true God? That's why he went on a search for truth, and tried to completely wipe his plate of anything religious he had ever learned.

(Phil) *About two years prior to this, I started having doubts. I had been questioning religion in general, but as I look back I believe I was questioning God. The same questions were whirling around in my mind that I hear people ask me now, and most can be summed up as this: "If there is an all-good God, why does He allow so many bad things to happen in this world?" I looked around and it seemed that there were highly intelligent people on both sides of the argument, and I thought "What hope do I have?" I would never be able to learn enough "book knowledge" to be able to understand, let alone debate with, some of these great minds; yet there was something inside of me that told me that if there was a God who actually created me, then He would lead me to the truth. Truth has to come from the source.*

I made a commitment that if He was there, listening, I would follow the truth no matter what He showed me. So I started researching the oldest known written religions, to the newest, the largest to the smallest, and everything in between. I started with the history, the facts, the myths, and read through the various translations that I could get my hands on. I started each day researching with the same prayer: "God, if you're there and this is the truth, show me; if not, show me why it's not." I had the same issues with most of the religions - only one person, only one vision, no witnesses, contradictions, lack of historical evidence, etc. The reading and researching always ended with me saying the same words - an overwhelming, "Nope, Next". I wasn't giving God credit for this, I just simply felt these were the logical conclusions anyone would come to. I saved the Bible for the last, since I had grown up on it and felt I already heard everything it had to say. At the end of the day, I still don't believe it was the reading, researching, logic or evidence; it was simply asking, knocking, and seeking.

Truth does come from the source – there are no magic words or special prayer, but simple faith and seeking. Hebrews 11:6 says, "But without faith it is impossible to please him: for he that cometh to God must believe that he is, and that he is a rewarder of them that diligently seek him." You may doubt if it was God who stopped the rain that night; sometimes I do too. But one thing that I do know is God opened my eyes to see the truth, and my heart to know the truth and my life hasn't been the same since I asked for forgiveness and surrendered my life to Him.

CHAPTER 20: REAL ESTATE AND AN ALL-IN PRAYER

I can't recall exactly how much time had passed before we finally told someone what had happened, but it was at least a year. We were in Ohio sharing a vacation home with Phil's five brothers and sisters, their spouses and kids and his parents. It was the Fourth of July and it was rare that all the families could get together. Phil and I went for a walk around the farm house and I told him, "I think we should tell your family what happened." "No," Phil said. "I don't think we need to tell anybody." "No," I said. I think we need to tell your family." "He said "No, I don't think we need to." I told him, "I don't agree, and we need to tell them what happened." So later that night, sitting around the bonfire, we shared what had happened to us. Some of his family cried, including Phil, as we both shared our side of what had happened. This was only the second time I had ever seen Phil cry in all our years together. Phil's little brother, Joey, came up to us privately that night and said He had been praying for something from God to wake us all up spiritually and bring us back to God together.

Before this night, Phil and I had kept what happened to ourselves, only whispering about it together for no one else to hear. Very, very slowly through the next year I shared it with a few people. I wouldn't want to, but I had to. I can remember a roofer, who was fulfilling a contract on our house, sitting on my couch before the job. His name was Stephan and we were just laughing and talking about our crazy party days (my normal conversation with anyone I met). He was talking and all I kept hearing over and over in my head was, "Tell him about the rain, Danny. Tell him about the rain." Having a God conversation about the crazy rain story was not what I wanted. I wanted to talk about the funny, stupid days of the past. But there it was again, playing like an old skipped record. "Tell him about the rain, Danny. Tell him about the rain." Fi-

110

nally, I couldn't take it anymore. My mouth was being forced and my tongue felt like it was being squeezed. And there it was: "Hey, I have something crazy to tell you about this rain one night." And just like that, I had told my first stranger.

Phil and I both decided soon after it happened that maybe God was trying to tell us something and maybe we should try making it to church more, because if He is trying to say something to us at least we would be making an effort to hear it. Phil also said he was going to be praying and that I should too, that our eyes would be open to see whatever God wanted to show us. I can't remember joining Phil on this. This was his rain thing that happened, not mine. I figured God is really real now and He will be showing Phil something someday. But as time passed we would not think about the rain very much, just once in a while, and that's also how often we would talk about it.

Well, my mom and I were hanging out together one day when Phil came home and said, "Hey, girls! My boss wants me to move to Minnesota again." We never wanted to move, and always laughed about these offers in the past, but this time without a second thought, we both said, "Sure! Let's get to selling the house." We had no idea what he had decided and prayed about...

(Phil) *I had been working for a healthcare company in their IT for about twelve years in Omaha. The Omaha office didn't grow much over those twelve years, but the Minneapolis division had been exploding. I wore many IT hats over the twelve years and, as the company grew, my various responsibilities started shrinking. I had been offered several positions as the new departments were started in Minnesota, but I always turned them down, not wanting to move (especially to anywhere colder). Growing up, we were constantly moving. It seemed like I would just start to make new friends, then come home to find my parents packing again. By the time I moved out of my parents' house, I didn't want to ever move again. Every time I was offered a position, my answer was always the same. "I'll take the job, but I will never ever, ever move to Minnesota".*

After the rain, my prayers changed from "Show me the truth" to "I'll do and go wherever it is you want me to go." I knew it was never going to be Minnesota though. One day I got an offer, and once again it was mandatory that I move to Minnesota. Without even a hesitation, I said, "I'll take the job, but I'm not moving to Minnesota." The boss said, "Why don't you think it over and let me know? I thought, "I did just let you know!" On the way home, I remembered what I had been praying: "If there is anything you want me to do or anywhere you want me to go, I'll do it, I'll go." I thought, "Oh no. Not Minnesota." I prayed and told God, "If you want me to go to Minnesota, you are going to get my wife and mother-in-law on board, because I can't move without them." I thought that should do it, since they wanted to move less than me. When I pulled in the driveway, they were already standing there waiting to greet me. Just like I had done so many times before, I relayed the job offer ever so nonchalantly, knowing they were going to brush this off without a second thought ... their response made my heart sink."

Our house was a weird home for a fast sale in the real estate market. First of all, I refused to use a realtor to sell the house, even at three percent commission, because it just didn't make sense to me to hire someone to sell our home, and Phil's boss told us to take all the time we needed to sell and move north. I needed a lot of time, because not only was our house a weird set-up, but I had planned to live there forever and had painted and decorated it as my own and in my own strange taste.

My bathroom was five different sponged colors to resemble a sunset, from the top canary yellow all the way to the floor, changing with orange and red. I collected a bit and the house was full of knick-knack stuff, so everything had to go to stage the home. The entire inside had to be painted normal home colors to be presentable to sell. It also had a huge in-law apartment that was slightly more up-to-date than the rest of the home. So who ever was going to buy it would be someone who really loved the people living in the apartment connected to it.

I got the house ready and staged and would advertise and show it every weekend. We had two cats that we would remove during the showings, so Phil and the kids would hide on the side street in the Tahoe with the cats and read books, while I played realtor in a business suit. It was hilarious and we really made the best of it. After about one year, it started to wear on us and his work finally said it was time to move up - but our house wasn't selling. It was a bad time to sell, the worst in years, and we were trying to sell an older house and the most expensive house on our block.

My mom was a Keno lady at Brewski's bar and had placed a flyer on her Keno counter. A woman came to her line and inquired about the flyer. That lady came in to view our home and she threw herself on my mom's bed in the apartment. She said she believed in God and that it was God's fate for her to buy this house - and she was going to buy it. Honestly, I thought she was drinking or something; but within a few weeks she bought the house. We moved to Minnesota the same week that Phil's boss gave him a deadline day to be up there by - it was within a twenty-four-hour period of the close of our Omaha property. It was crazy. You're going to be hearing me say that too many times, but honestly life just gets crazier from this point.

(Phil) After I accepted the new position, *the first thing my new boss said was I needed to be up in Minnesota by July 2011; that only gave us a month to get the house in selling shape, on the market and sold. I said OK, because I figured if God wanted us up there somehow all of this would work out. Before my deadline to be up there, that boss was transferred to a different role and the new boss had a completely different attitude. He said*

"Take your time. However long it takes is fine." Every other week when we met for our one-on-one meetings, it was the same response: "How's the house selling going? Don't worry about moving up here - however long it takes is fine." We begin to pray more as a family and started to teach the kids to trust God, and that He would move us when He was ready for us to move. We showed the house for a year, without one single offer, not one. In June of 2012, I met with my boss for our one-on-one meeting and, without warning; the conversation took a 180-degree turn. "You know the new equipment you need to support is hitting the docks next month?" he said. "Sure," I replied. "Well, you need to be up here to support it - what are you going to do about it?" he asked. I had no idea. I thought maybe I could travel up there for the week and back home on the weekends to see the family for a while until we figured out plan B. I promised the kids that God had a plan, and whatever that was we were going to do it. We were selling the house just to break even, and didn't even have a single offer, but in less than 30 days after meeting with my boss, the house was sold, and we were moving into a house in Minnesota.

We moved up on July 5th, 2012, in one of the worst heat spells Minnesota has ever had. It was so hot and it took us all night to unload the truck that was due back the next morning. To save some money, we moved ourselves instead of hiring anyone. My mother was a bit of a hoarder and she had what seemed like thousands of tiny boxes, and unfortunately so did I. I had no experience moving and I did not pack in large boxes either. But we got through it all and got cozy in our temporary home. We spent the next 3 months going to 30 different lakes and exploring everything we could in Minnesota.

Soon after we got to our rental in Apple Valley, Minnesota, we found a school for the kids (who were now both in third grade), and a church called River Valley. River Valley is a wonderful church speaking a solid message and transforming the world with their Global Teams. It also helped that they had plenty of free donuts and coffee. Phil would still go into the kid's bedroom and say prayers with them at night, and it still seemed a little weird to me. I went in most of the time but I remember thinking, "Oh great, we will end up with those weird church kids who have no fun in life."

I wasn't upset about it, I just remember that thought going through my mind one day. It was a stereotype that I placed on church kids, especially middle and upper-class church kids, because now that we moved to Apple Valley, it seemed we were being considered upper middle class. I considered the houses around us all rich white people houses, with Stepford Wives in them. I tried to make friends at the bus stop with the moms, but we really didn't have much in common. I was the ghetto one with a Pontoon in the driveway. I even remember one of the neighborhood moms mentioning how tacky it is for people to park their boats in the driveways – and our boat was in our driveway. I still made an effort to be social, but I felt lonely in the new neighborhood.

A very odd thing started to happen the moment we moved up here from Omaha. Phil and I would go out of the house and these strangers would randomly come up to us and start talking to us about God. It seemed like it was happening at least once every other week wherever we went. I just figured Minnesota must have more Bible thumpers than Omaha did or had more Bible college kids graduating from here. We were still regularly going to the church at River Valley in Apple Valley, when one Sunday they passed out an "All in Prayer" on a postcard to everyone in the church. I didn't give it much notice but it read something like this: "God, I surrender my life completely to you and ask every day for your will to be done in my life before my own." Now I am paraphrasing, but that was the gist of it.

Later, Phil and I were in our kitchen when I pulled the folded-up postcard out of my pocket. It was a seven-day all-in prayer challenge to the whole church. I asked him if he was going to do it. He said, "Sure." We talked about it because we were both a little frightened of it. Phil said something about, "Well, I don't want God to tell me he wants me to go to Korea and get my head cut off." We chuckled a bit and I said, "Yeah, I don't want to be one of those crazy people." We talked about it a little longer, and then I remember telling him to just say it then. Phil was kind of playing and kind of serious when he started to read the prayer. When he got to the part about "God's will be done in my life before my own will", He pretended as if the words couldn't roll out of his mouth, like in the movies when someone is forced to say something they don't want to say. We laughed and I gave him a hard time, and then he said it. I said the prayer also and nothing happened. The earth didn't open up nor did an angel appear in our kitchen. But we both agreed to start the prayer challenge. I was sure nothing would happen, but I know Phil was a little nervous something might.

CHAPTER 21: TERRACOTTA WARRIORS AND WORDS FROM GOD

We were going out that Friday, because our friend Jake Ellenberger was going to fight in the UFC and on Pay per View. So we headed out to Carbone's in Apple Valley to eat pizza and have some drinks while we cheered our friend on. It was cool because we had trained a little with Jake and to see him make it to the UFC was a big deal for us. I dressed very sexy as usual, with my knee-high, fur-lined, laced-up, four-inch heel leather boots, my skinny jeans and a sexy top. My long, chocolate 'Victoria Secret' hair was curled to perfection. We sat at the bar and as our friend was fighting I was tossing punches in the air and yelling, "Kick his ass, Jake." Suddenly a guy standing between and behind both Phil and me tapped me on the shoulder. He asked me about the fighter, and then started telling me about God.

I tapped Phil and he was telling us both about God and the Bible and those we needed to pray for Syria and Israel. Now, Phil and I were holding each other and we were drinking and cheering our boy on the TV, so this seemed very strange, but we had both started the all-in prayer and we were going to give this guy a conversation. I remember getting up to use the bathroom and when I looked in the mirror, dressed the way I was dressed, I couldn't believe anyone would approach us to talk about God with us as we sat at the bar screaming at the TV. I went into the stall and prayed. I had been drinking, but my head was one hundred percent sober. I told God I was listening if He was there. I went back out and Phil and I talked to this guy for an hour. Our whole fight night turned into an all-about-God night right there at the very busy bar. It was weird, but when the guy first spoke to me my face felt like it was so hot; the words felt like they were pushing into my face.

Phil and I talked about how strange the whole thing was. The guy wasn't drunk or anything - why did he do that? We both brushed it off as a strange coincidence, lining up with us doing the all-in prayer challenge. That next Tuesday, Phil took off work while the kids were in school, so the two of us could go check out the Minneapolis Institute of Arts. They had a special display of the Terracotta Warriors, and both Phil and I wanted to go check them out. I think we had both read about the buried life-sized warriors as kids and we loved walking around this museum. So we planned a day date together. It wasn't often we did stuff without the kids, but we were planning a romantic day. I remember Phil was getting ready, taking a shower as I stood outside the shower curling my hair. I was a little sad - I had just received a rejection from the first modeling and acting agency I had auditioned for.

I cried when it came in the mail saying "Thanks, but no thanks". I wasn't used to rejection letters. It hurt so I was pouting about it. I was telling Phil, "We have lived here for months now and I still haven't picked up anything for work. I just want to start making some money," I said to him. "I know," Phil said, "but staying here right now you don't have to even make any money. We are covering our entire bills just fine." "I know we are," I said. "But I want to do something to make extra money to help for the down payment we are going to need when we find a house. Or even if we want to go on vacation." Phil said, "Look, I know you want to get busy but just take it easy for now, if you are looking for something gratifying to do, you could volunteer. One of my co-workers Rick came in on a Monday and he was shining. I ask him what had happened and he told me he had the best weekend he ever had. He proceeded to tell me how he went downtown with this crazy Jesus guy name Scott and volunteered with the homeless." This was not something I wanted to do.

"I do not want to volunteer," I said. "Those people don't get paid." I would do good deeds like feed starving children and help strangers out, but never regularly volunteer. That made no sense to me at all. I said, "Look, we do good deeds all the time. I don't need to go out and regularly volunteer." He said playfully, "Oh, maybe you are supposed to pray about that!"

We had been sarcastically telling each other to pray about things. So I said playfully and very arrogantly, "Fine, I will!" I put my curling iron down and threw my arms out, tilting my head back and face up to God. I said, "God, if you're listening, I want you to know if you want me to volunteer or anything crazy like that, then you better just hit me in the head with a two-by-four with a clear sign from you that that's what you want me to do. Amen." I opened my eyes, picked my curling iron back up and flirtatiously told Phil, "There. I did it." We both chuckled about it and Phil got out of the shower. As He went in to get dressed, I reminded him about these Bible thumpers who kept coming out of the woodwork at us and that we should try to avoid them today. Phil walked out from the closet with a black t-shirt on with two white skulls and white flames coming off it and said, "How's this? You think this will keep them away?" I said I hoped so.

We were feeling very carefree and being very playful with each other. When we got in our car, the conversation got a little serious and we started talking about God and the Bible. We talked about all these people who kept popping out at us and talking God stuff to us. We talked about the rain that day and all the strange things that happened, like the way the house sold and the "all-in" praying we had been doing. Phil said, "All I know is God is real and we are supposed to be here in Minnesota."

I said, "I know, but you had the rain thing happen to you. I guess I'll just need my own rain story." "Be careful what you ask for," Phil said. We talked all the way about God and the Bible. I was filled with doubts and just had a hard time wrapping my mind around God really existing that day. We were still talking about it as we got out of the car. We had pulled into a large parking garage for the Arts Theater and parked in the street level.

We got out and were now walking hand in hand to the large grass courtyard that led to the doors of the giant building. I stopped and as I looked down at the long sidewalk we were on, I took my foot and pointed with my toes to the line in the pathway that divides each section in all sidewalks. I said, "You see this line?" I took my right foot and only allowed my pinky side of my shoe to cross the side of the line leaving the rest of my foot on the other side of the line.

"I am a toe-in-the-water believer; I've given my life to Christ and we go to church and do good deeds, but if God wants me to be an all-in believer, I guess I will have to have my own sign from God." I continued and jumped over the line and said, "A sign where I take my hands and throw them in the air and say, 'OK, I get it now. You're real and I know what you want me to do." I actually did the actions and put my hands in the air as we stood completely alone on the sidewalk along the side of the Arts Theater. Phil again said, "Yeah, I know what you mean. All I can tell you is when you ask God something and He gives you an answer, there will be no doubt and you will throw your hands up and say 'OK, I get it!'"

Our conversation switched as we got around people and we went back to flirting with each other. We entered into the Arts Theater and headed towards the area we would find the Terracotta Warrior display. We got directions from the front desk because this place was huge. It was hard to stay on track to the Warrior section because of all the cool stuff to look at. We would get distracted and look at art and read it.

All the time we were kissing or holding hands. I remember feeling very romantic that day, constantly giving Phil little pecks on the cheek or lips. We paused alone in a room and I nudged him and pointed up with a nod of my head for Phil to look at what I am looking at. He looked up and it was a picture of Jesus and his disciples at the Last Supper. I leaned in close and whispered, "Look, it's a picture of Jesus. It must be my sign." We both smirked and then the smirk turned into a smile. We continued to pause and go as we made our way to the special viewing area for the Terracotta Warriors. As we got to the back counter, we paid to enter this part and also paid a few bucks more for headphones to guide us along our tour. When we entered the first of four rooms, we synchronized our headphones to start at the exact same second so we could listen together. We are dorks and we truly love each other that much. There was a display in the center of the room that we would slowly make our way full circle around as we listened about the details of the display. I looked up once and saw a guy standing in the corner wearing a suit.

I knew he was there to make sure we didn't touch anything or go past the ropes. He was younger than us, maybe mid-to-late twenties, with black hair, and he made eye contact with me. I am sure I probably smiled. I smile at everyone and am a very happy-go-lucky person, and today I was filled with joy and peace. He smiled back and as our session ended for this room we exited into the second of four rooms. Phil and I made our way around the art and halfway I looked up again and there he was, the same guy standing in the same corner watching the group of people. We caught eyes again and I gave him a slightly confused face.

I looked behind me to confirm to myself that I had in fact switched rooms, and I had. So I looked back at the guy and I realized, with my background of working retail that this guy must be on a room rotation. I nodded and smiled at him and mouthed, "You guys switch rooms?" I took my hands and made a switch front/back with them and he smiled and nodded his head. I smirked and nodded my head as if to say, "I get it, at least I know I'm not crazy." In most places in retail or in boring jobs they rotate the workers to keep them fresh and so they are moving once in a while. If you stood in one spot all day, you would hate your job or fall asleep standing up. Once, I was on a twenty-minute rotation as a dealer and switching tables constantly kept us more tuned in to our environment and meant fewer mistakes on the tables.

I immediately went back into focusing on the Warriors and holding Phil's back pockets or hand. In the next room, I saw the kid but paid no mind to him. Then finally Phil and I made it to the fourth and final room still hand in hand. As our tour entered we exited, but just past the door Phil stopped and said, "I want to go back in the last room one more time." I agreed and we walked in. I still had my headphones on my ears and as I reentered the room I stood looking at Phil, who was right in front of me looking at the Warrior in the center of the room. On my left was the guy again.

He was standing right next to me, looking forward also. I figured I should at least make small talk as he was about a foot to my left. So I took the headphones off and said, "So did you get stuck working Thanksgiving or do you guys close for that?" He seemed really happy to answer and said, "No, it's closed on the Holiday." I said, "Good for you." He nodded towards Phil saying, "You two are pretty into these Terracotta Warriors, aren't you?" I said, "Yeah, we saw them as kids on TV." He said, "Yep, I can tell. I can also tell you two are down with the Bible." I said, confused, "We are what?"

This guy was smiling and positively nodding his head and said, "I can tell you two are down with the Bible." I realized what he was saying and was frozen in my tracks. I said, "What are you talking about?" He said, "You two are beaming with it, you are glowing with it." As he excitedly said this to me, I remembered all the God talk Phil and I had had in private about an hour ago now and was shocked. I said, "Stop! What are you talking about?" He had a huge smile on his face and said, "Spirit recognizes spirit and I can tell you two believe in the Bible - it's all over your faces. Look around you; look at all the other people."

When I looked up, I could see all the other people like I always see other people - full of pain and insecurities and looking lost. I looked back at the kid and he said, "I can't talk about it much here at work because I will get into trouble, but spirit recognizes spirit and I am supposed to tell you that you are supposed to volunteer and you're supposed to volunteer downtown." He lifted his hand and started to name places. Touching a finger on his right hand each time, he named a place like a child would do when learning to count ... one ... two ... three. His voice faded out as my face started burning up and tears were flowing down my cheeks. I couldn't believe what I was hearing.

Unfortunately, at this time I had kind of lost control of my body. I couldn't hear what he was saying over my own panic and disbelief over what was happening right now. I had never fainted or blacked out in my life. I felt like I was about to. I turned away and started to panic and motion to Phil, who was five feet from me by now, to come over. Phil saw my hand softly at my side calling him over and was annoyed because I was going to make him talk to someone. Phil hated talking to new people. When he saw my face he was extremely concerned, "What is going on?" I said through my tears, and barely made it through the words, "Would you please tell my husband what you just said to me?"

The guy was so excited, he looked to the left and then back to Phil and said, "I told her I can't talk about it here at work but spirit recognizes spirit and the Holy Spirit is moving, and I told her she needed to volunteer downtown." Phil and the guy said a few more quick things and I started walking out of the room in a panic. I was bawling my eyes out and Phil walked out with me. We made it about 15 steps away and I turned to him and he held me. I cried out loud and then started to softly giggle through my tears. My hands were quivering in joy and fear as

I reached them up to the ceiling with people walking all around us. I said quietly, "OK, I get it now. I know you are real and I know what you want me to do." I was full of feelings that I had never felt before. At that second, I knew my life was over as I had known it. I knew I was done with my wants and dreams of being famous and rich and now I was going to be one of those goofy Bible people, and I was completely OK with it. I went into the bathroom and realized I was not dying anytime soon because God had something he wanted me to do. I cried out loud in the bathroom alone, because I couldn't believe the God of the universe could possibly want to use me for anything.

I was not a good person, I hated church, and boasted once about all the sins I had committed, including my abortions. I didn't know why he would want to use me for anything, but I was a hundred percent sure that God was real, and I was supposed to volunteer downtown. I was in shock as we left for our car. We went to the parking lot discussing frantically what had just happened.

CHAPTER 22: SCOTT STOVER AND THE STREET TEAM

On our way home, we knew my mom would be there to greet our two kids at the bus stop, but we also knew that our best friends from Omaha were coming into town to see us. I couldn't get my head together. I just wanted to go home and for the first time in my whole life, I wanted to read the Bible - because I knew it was real. I wanted to see what it had to say. I just couldn't pretend like this didn't happen and pop open a bottle with our friends and chit chat all night. I was too shaken up.

We arrived home and told my mom and the kids what had happened. They had already heard about the rain story, but were too young to get how crazy it was. Dan and Rebecca and their two daughters were already pulling into the driveway, and for a few seconds I pretended like everything was normal. We walked into the kitchen and I leaned my back against the kitchen sink. As the kids ran around greeting each other, I looked at our best friends of 14 years and told them what just happened. I was quivering and Phil helped me get through it.

Dan grew up going to the same church Phil went to, and Rebecca went to a similar church as well. At his church, I felt judged by your way I wore my hair and clothes, and I felt guilty as a sinner unworthy of their church the second I walked in the door. It was an uncomfortable place and I had only been there once or twice, but as far as I knew Dan and Beck were not really into it and had only gone as kids because their parents made them. As far as I remember, we had never discussed God or the Bible in all the years we'd hung out and partied together. Every weekend for the past five years, we would play cards all night and sleep over each at other's houses; our kids were best friends with their kids and had grown up together.

As I stood telling them in the kitchen that God is real, I cried in front of them for the first time. Big Dan got a tear in his eye and came over and hugged me. Then when I finished, Rebecca also had tears in her eyes and said, "Isn't it awesome? I remember when I first realized God was real, and it is sort of like having a new boyfriend. Like when you are all excited to have a relationship and it's all new. Just like a relationship, it will have its ups and downs and many different feelings. Just understand that this new part with the butterflies in the stomach could fade away."

I couldn't believe anyone I ever knew could have felt the way I felt at this second. I couldn't believe that others had this knowledge and weren't running around yelling it on the roof tops every second of every day. I would come to understand this, a lot better as time passed. We hung out for the next 5 days together, but things had already started to change in me.

I didn't feel like getting drunk and being the "funny, crazy, get-the-party-started" Danny I was known for. I just wanted to go pray and read the Bible to see if God had anything else to tell me. I walked through the week with our company, but would go to bed really early to go pray and read the Bible. That Sunday we went to the same "rich people church" we had been going to. We both decided we would just keep praying and telling God we would do anything he wants us to, but the direction would have to be so clear we would know beyond the shadow of any doubt that it was God's way.

At the River Valley Church, we went into a side room where you can talk to a member. I started crying and babbling, telling them what had happened last week and that I was supposed to volunteer downtown. They pointed us to a member's dinner, and the small group website. We went to the dinner and sat with a bunch of young kids surrounded by hundreds of people; we ate and I told someone about the crazy thing that happened at the Arts Theater.

(Phil) *The move to Minnesota was a huge deal for me. I absolutely hated moving and thought this was a miracle for me to be here. Over the years, I had withdrawn from talking with people, new people most of all. There was very little I liked doing less than meeting someone new. I felt an aching in my chest, some call it anxiety, but whatever it is I wanted no part of it and knew that wasn't for me. I would do what God wanted me to do, but it was going to be behind the scenes - maybe cleaning the church after everyone was gone or something without human interaction. When Danny got "hit in the head with the two by four", I thought that was going to be great for her, and I was thinking "I'm glad I didn't pray that". God, and Danny, apparently had a different idea. We started to look around for somewhere for her to volunteer, but nothing jumped out. Right then, Rick Praire, my co-worker, invited me to a Friday night outreach that he had gone to a couple of weeks prior, with Scott Stover. I tried to wriggle my way out of it, saying I needed to do something with Danny, and would let him know. Once again God was already meeting me off at the pass and I had no idea. Danny and I went to River Valley and tried to volunteer for anything they had. They pointed us to their small group website and we started reading through. One looked like it was for couples, a volunteering opportunity downtown, and we wouldn't have to drive ourselves. It seemed like it was going to be an easy in-and-out operation.*

One small detail, that I glanced right over... they meet up with a guy from a different church named Scott Stover. Before we knew it, we were in a van with a bunch of people I didn't know, heading to a city with a lot more people I didn't know, and I was secretly hoping we ended up in a ditch instead. I thought that would definitely be a better end to this night than what this was looking like. My chest was aching, and I knew this was going to be a disaster, but having surrendered this over to Him, I just let go of the steering wheel and told Him that He needed to take control of this night.

I made Phil go. Phil objected, saying it was God's message for me not him, but I wasn't having it. He was going if I was going. So we went to this church called Community of Hope out in Rosemount, where we met Scott and Rick. Rick was Phil's co-worker who told him about this thing he did on Friday night and had been asking Phil to go. We prayed in a circle and it was kind of weird, but nice. We got into a van and I shared what happened to the two guys. They knew God was real too, and had tons of crazy stories like mine. We went to ICCM church on 1812 Park Ave downtown. I was so nervous because I knew God wanted me here and was scared and excited about what might happen.

The church was very small, like an old office building; it was flat and long on the outside and sat right next to an old brick apartment building called The Waldorf. There was music playing quietly and it was very dark inside. There was a microphone in front of the stage with maybe ten people randomly seated in the fold-out chairs on the floor in a U shape all around the front of the stage. The microphone was lit up, but the faces of the people were hard to see. I went out from the kitchen where we had entered with a cooler from Community of Hope that we had brought, and some hot dog buns and chips. We brought the stuff in and Phil and I were encouraged by Scott to go in and have a seat anywhere. So we sat in the dark, somewhere where no one would notice us.

I don't remember who prayed or what they prayed for, but one by one, strangers would go up to the microphone and take it from its stand. They would cry and pray to God. It was addiction and pain-filled prayers. When the hot dogs were done boiling in the kitchen, Scott and Rick called us back and the four of us drained them and wrapped them in a bun and then foil. We placed about a hundred of them in a cooler and loaded them up in the white van we had drove down together in. We headed out and I was so nervous; I had no idea what to expect. We went to an underpass off the interstate and we all were excited. Scott called out to see if there was anyone, but said it was too cold

- so we headed to a shelter. Scott showed us where people were staying and shared with us some of the stories of people he had met.

We made our way to an inner-city men's shelter and we were given permission by the guards to go in. We walked into what looked like a large high school cafeteria, but instead of cafeteria tables there were rows and rows of bunk beds. There were maybe ten to fifteen rows of bunk beds, eight beds long. Each row backed up to the row next to it so it was almost like the beds had dividers of a thin two-foot wall between the men lying in them. There were guys all over the place; the floor was lined with every type of person you could think of - Asian, Black, Sudanese, Jamaican, White, Mexican. There was not an ethnicity I didn't see. I could hear them talking and whispering, and some were fighting.

There were some sad, some happy, some mad, some were suspicious while others were quite welcoming. There were some clean and some dirty and some seemed vicious while others so sweet. It was a mix of so many different types of men. We put the cooler on the table - forty percent left their bunks or spots on the floor and formed a line at the cooler. They were all so grateful for the hot dogs and chips. I just kept smiling and saying, "God bless you" and handed chips out. When we handed out all the food, I noticed a guy. He was white and in his early twenties. I started talking to him and he asked me if I could pray for him. Before I knew what was happening, I had my hand in his hand, and the other rested on his shoulder, and prayer was coming out of my mouth.

I told every guy I could that God is really real and he loves you, and shared God's plan of salvation. I told them what happened to me and why I was standing in front of them now, because God told me to. Phil was over somewhere doing the same thing. Now I had never in my life heard people pray for people like this. I never circled up in prayer or even had someone pray over me, so for me to be praying with these men, it was absolutely crazy that this was happening. Some men were beaten, bloodied and bruised. Some cried, but most everyone was sad and lonely. Some seemed completely cuckoo for coco puffs, and others were in a fight with their girl or just arrived from another city.

All of them had their own story and all of them seemed to find comfort from the attention they received from the four of us. We left and made our way together in the van and discussed who we'd met and what prayers were said. We were all filled with excitement from the whole experience and sat and chatted for a while in the van after we got back to the suburbs. Phil and I talked a little on the way home about the guys we met and what they had said. When we arrived at our rental property out in Apple Valley and took off our gear, we were both really hungry but too tired to go into the kitchen. We sat down on the couch together in complete silence.

I looked over into the kitchen towards the refrigerator and thought about all my options. I thought about how full my refrigerator was and that I had anything I could want to possibly eat at this second in it, and I was humbled. I looked at the TV in front of me, and the warm three-thousand-square-foot home we were living in and was humbled. I thought about my two beautiful, healthy, and smart children snuggled up in their own bedrooms and in their own beds, and was embarrassed at how much we had and was, once more, humbled. I turned my head to Phil and said what we were both thinking: "Our lives are never going to be the same again." Phil softly smiled and nodded his head in agreement. We both knew we were forever changed and this was exactly where God wanted us to be, both of us. Phil said, "We've had so many great nights, but this was the best night we ever had".

You see, I think Phil is educated in the word of the Bible and I know I am not. I was comfortable speaking to anyone and anywhere and Phil was not. Together we seemed to be a great match for sharing Christ.

God knew after my childhood I was comfortable to sit on a mat under a bridge in filth with a homeless man and laugh and pray with him. He also knew Phil would fall away from not wanting to meet new people and become just like the social kid he was while growing up. God knew I would tell the whole world what happened to me. And to this day, I haven't stopped, and nothing has ever felt better or more right.

CHAPTER 23: VIETNAM AND VELVET CAKE

I kind of felt a bit like Alice falling down the hole; just like we had stepped out of our own world and entered into a crazy world full of amazing 'God experiences'. As soon as we both hopped on board to the Friday Night street team to downtown Minneapolis, neither one of us could even imagine ever missing a Friday night. We thought about it all week long. Phil got plugged into a men's group where they would meet once a week and talk about God stuff. He would come home and tell me these crazy stories he would hear in his men's Bible group, one story in particular was an older man who shared his Vietnam story....

(Phil) *I was meeting at a Men's Bible Study group; one night the question was asked if God was still in the miracle-making business today, like the stories we read about in the Bible. Our leader was an old Vietnam vet and spoke up without hesitation and told us this story. He was a medic on a two-man team, always rotating one on the gunner - one making the run to retrieve the downed man. This time it was his turn to run, and when he reached his injured soldier, he needed to perform a trachea since the man was drowning on his own blood. While he was making the incision, he heard his partner fire up the gunner from the helicopter door, he looked around and didn't see any enemies coming, and so put his head back down and went back to work. Once he finished inserting the tube he picked up the man and started running back to the chopper; all the while, his partner was burning through shells. Once back in the air and the firing stopped, his partner looked like he was in shock and said, "What was that? Who were they? He said, "What are you talking about?" His partner said, "All those men in white surrounding you; they stopped the bullets from the snipers in the trees that were firing on you." He said, "I didn't see them, but it's like I've been telling you - God is real, and I pray to Jesus to keep us safe*

*every time you go out and every time I go out, and I know that was God's
angels watching over us today."*

As I continued to hear these incredible stories, I couldn't help but think
it was like some huge secret people were only comfortable sharing with
other believers in small church groups. I would think to myself, "Well,
what good does that do?" How much would I have to dislike someone
to not tell them what had happened to me and that God was real and
so is heaven? These crazy "Godcidences" kept happening, over and over
again. We coined the word (Godcidence), one night on street team and
now we all use it regularly. We use it when something happened that we
know was not an ordinary coincidence and it was obviously for God's
purpose. You are welcome to take it and use it too! This seemed to be
happening so much, that even our two kids couldn't help but take notice. Phil and I continued to pray every day, for God to use us for his
purpose whatever it may be, and it seemed like every time we turned
around people searching for God were coming right to us. This happened everywhere at the grocery store, the bowling alley, and even at a
hidden fishing spot.

They seemed to bring up the conversation, we just seemed to hang out
and wait. It was absolutely amazing to us. You would think I must have
had a cross around my neck or a Bible under my arm. Everywhere we
went, there they were. The more we plugged in, the deeper and more
often God used us to share Christ with strangers.

The second or third time on the street team, we went out with a large
group of men from a suburb church. Most of them seemed a bit scared,
but were committed to the project because they had signed up to go
out on a street team at their church. We had so much to give away that
night it was awesome. I had been out at least once on the street team,
but already felt led to lead some of the men to put tables out and how to
form the lines and pass out food and flyers. Scott, Rick, and Phil left the

corner parking lot where we were set up to go and advertise to the community that we were there. The men I was with, about thirty of them, were wonderful and were giving their best, although most seemed uncomfortable. I stepped out into the line to offer prayer and then some men joined me. The night was a huge success and a lot of homeless men women and children received boots and coats since it was winter and freezing out.

I saw Phil show back up with an older woman whose arms were full of stuff, and that stuff was all she had to her name. Phil was trying to convince her to let him hold her belongings so she could get a hot dog and hot cocoa. But she wasn't having it. Later, when the night was over, Phil told me the full story of his encounter with her. He had found her down the street and invited her back for food and drink. It took him several attempts before she would succumb and when she finally looked at him she said, "Oh, I remember you!" "You're that guy from last week who gave me the red velvet cake." She continued, "I was just on the next street over and you were driving that convertible car and you jumped out and gave me the red velvet cake. It was so good! I am so glad you came back - I wanted to thank you again."

Phil said he was shaking his head the whole time and said, "No, I have never been over here before and this is only my second time ever doing anything like this. You must have me mixed up with someone else." "No", she said angrily, "you just don't remember. I know it was you." Phil said, "I'm sorry, but I don't even own a convertible," and then she replied, "Oh, you're an idiot and you just don't remember. It was the other night and you were stopped at a red light. You jumped out of the car and ran over to give me a piece of red velvet cake. I could never forget it was you because I knew when I saw your face; I could never forget your eyes." Phil smiled and shrugged his shoulders, thinking she was crazy she said, "Don't worry. You'll remember. I know it was you. I'll never forget your eyes."

When Phil told me this, I knew instantly that what she saw was Christ's love in him - just as she had seen it in the guy who did jump out at that red light with cake in his hands, and just as those men who came out with us shone with the love of Jesus. The broken-hearted see the same person in each of us and don't even notice our own flesh. We are one in Christ and I wrote this out to share instantly with all the men who had been a part of God's plan that night. It didn't matter if you just stood there and smiled while handing out hot dogs or if you were on your knees praying with them. It didn't matter if you were the person who paid for the hot dogs or donated used socks but couldn't come out with us. We are all one in Christ, and God needs us all for our own part we play for his purpose - each and every one of us.

Everything I share with you now I was not taught or raised on. It is what God taught me in His church on the streets and in my home and work place by me surrendering to his will. So when you hear me say things that line up with God's word, the Bible, it is not because I knew it and then repeated it. It's because God opened my eyes to it, in prayer and obedience to Him. So it blows my mind every time something in our lives happens and the nugget of information I take out of it lines up with God's word. I have stumbled into all this, like a clumsy non-believing fool.

Maybe the fourth time we went out on the street team, there were at least six of us. We parked on Broadway and Lyndale and set up our tables across from the liquor store. It was an amazing night and we prayed with many people. We fed about one hundred and seventy-five, and also handed out whatever clothing and supplies we could collect that week. That night we had about five different people ask us if they went to this church we invited them to, if they would see us there. We all had our own churches we went to, so the answer was always the same. "No, sorry we don't go there." At the end of the night, we loaded up the white van and we were all seated inside with the lights off, chatting about our Godcidences. We noticed a very beautiful young black lady making her way across to our corner. Scott and I got back out and asked her where she was going. She simply said, "I don't know."

We asked her if she needed prayer; she started crying and said, "Yes." Now out on street team we always pointed people to the ICCM church, where we made the hot dogs up for street team. Now I had never been, other than the Friday night prayer night where we prepared the food. I knew it was a Bible-believing church that worked with people from all over the city in their struggles - sex abuse, prostitution, drug addictions, even the drug dealers. I heard the pastors there helped plant a Teen Challenge in Minnesota, and knew it was a place for people to get back what drugs and alcohol took from them. So I told her about the church and told her she should get plugged in there this Sunday.

She looked at me and said, "Will you be there?" "No," I said. By this time, Rick and Phil had gotten out of the van and were standing by us. She turned to Scott and said, "Will you be there?" Scott said, "Ah no, I go to Community of Hope." Then Scott and I looked at the rest of the team, and we realized no one on our team even went to that church. We were all from the suburbs. She turned and said, "Don't any of you go to that church?" Embarrassed, because we all knew the answer, we all shook our heads. Then she said, "I'll go. I'll go if all y'all go this Sunday!" Bug-eyed we stood and forced from our lips, "Sure ... we will go to that church too." Each one of us committed to her to go Sunday with our families.

Well, that Sunday my family of four headed about thirty minutes away to the Inner City Church of Minneapolis. I had never been there in the daytime, but I was fairly comfortable walking in. About an hour in, I noticed we may have been the only white family, but it was no big deal. We knew our kids being eight and nine years old at this time wouldn't take notice and, if they did, for sure wouldn't care.

Our family never even talked about different races differently. We raised our kids that we are just all people. Inside the church, there were really no windows, or at least not any light coming in; it seemed very dark compared to the well-lit and bright churches we went to. We definitely knew the neighborhood we were in, and there was no way I was going to take my kids to the kid's area and leave them - absolutely not! I was positive this place probably had no fire drill plan or even fire sprinklers for that matter. The kids area was somewhere in the basement. Absolutely not, I thought. They will be watching this service with us.

Scott, and Rick and their families showed up and we all sat together. The lady who we met on Friday also showed up with us because we picked her and her daughter up. I noticed a lady who appeared to be high on heroin but, again, coming from my background, it was something I had seen before and I felt comfortable with her. The churchgoers wore a wide variety of clothes. Some wore very loud colors, some overly sexy, but somehow seemed more normal than everyone dressing the same or "dressing to impress". No one was judging me here and I could feel that. When the music started, every seat in the house was empty, and everyone was standing, singing and clapping or arms raised in praise. The music was very alive and we were all sucked in right out of the gate. Angelo was to my left and he was clapping and dancing. We all had huge smiles on our faces because this somehow felt right. The music sounded great, I mean not like it was being played through high quality Bose speakers type of great, but the beat was so fun you couldn't help yourself.

About three songs in, the pastor came on to the stage and opened the altars for prayer. A lady in front of us wailed out in emotional pain and fell to the floor. Another woman from the church came over to hold the lady on the ground and whisper prayer into her ear. The pastor was a tiny white woman with a raspy radio DJ voice. Pastor Monica squeaked when she giggled and wore flaming 5-inch heels. One, I had never seen a girl pastor and two, she was a white lady and these people were all black. I would have thought it was going to be an old black guy.

Pastor Monica's husband Pastor Chris preached the sermon that day. It was fantastic and quick to the point. I really seemed to get it. At the end, Pastor Monica did what all Bible-based churches are supposed to do and she asked if there is anyone here who hasn't given their lives to Christ. She explained what it means like pastors usually do, but she explained it Pastor Monica's style. Now you should know that my son Angelo had been to church with us at least fifty times at this point and we had explained John 3:16 to him several times. Angelo is a very smart young man and I was sure he had prayed the "sinner's prayer" in Sunday School in the past. At the end of the service when Pastor Monica invited anyone who needs to surrender their lives to Christ before they walk out that door today, I felt a tugging and pushing on my left. I looked to see my son Angelo, with tears streaming down his cheeks and pushing passed me to get through the aisle. I punched Phil in the arm and pointed to Angelo, who was now between us and gave Phil a firm, "Go with your son" look and head nod. Phil threw his arms around Angelo and escorted him to the stage. Angelo gave his life to Christ that day at our first service at ICCM.

We dropped off the lady who had challenged us to be there and her daughter. All the way home Angelo kept repeating to us, "Dad, I get it now. John 3:16 – 'For God so loved the world that he gave his only son.' I get it, now it makes sense." Domiano said, "I just noticed that, we were like the only white people and why did that lady fall down crying?" I explained to her that we get to live in a perfect little bubble at this point in our lives. It has been a painless life and nothing bad has happened to us. Some people like that lady have had big pain and sad stuff happen. She fell because the pain was so great and she wanted God to take it." Later that night, Phil and I both agreed that we were supposed to be there at ICCM church, and we also agreed we would continue to go there unless God directed our steps elsewhere.

CHAPTER 24: MIRACLES AND THE LOCH NESS MONSTER

Phil and I were walking through life on high alert, looking for any opportunity to share Christ with strangers. I would tell Phil once in a while, "Hey, I think we are supposed to write down that rain story. He would say, "Oh, yeah," and that would be the end of it. Then a few days later I would say it again and Phil would give me the same dry answer. This went on for a while.

It just kept popping in my head and then out my mouth: "Hey, I think we are supposed to write down that rain story." But even if we were supposed to, we were both way too lazy and way too insecure in our writing ability to write it out. I don't know why, but one night Phil was sitting on our couch in Apple Valley and I said, "I think we are supposed to write down that rain story." Phil said, "OK" with the same zero intention to ever do it. With tears forming in my eyes I said, "I am sick and tired of telling you what God is telling me. We are supposed to do it and I don't even need to tell you anymore, because someone else is going to tell you." I was mad and sad and I still have no idea why I said what I said - it just ran out my mouth. It was an urgency to hurry up and do it and I have no idea why. Well the next day, Phil came home shaking his head. "You ain't going to believe what happened today at work," he said. He told me that he had never really shared the rain story with anybody outside of that one time with his family, especially anybody at his work. But about 4 months ago he had been working on a big problem with his co-worker Ted Blakley, and had been at work pushing twenty-four hours with hardly a break to eat or close his eyes. It was just him and Ted, stuck side by side for hours upon hours.

He didn't normally work with him like that, but it was a big outage and they were both dedicated to seeing the fix through. In a moment of exhaustion, with lack of clarity their conversation got personal and

Ted mentioned something about his cross key chain. Ted shared a God experience with Phil and asked if anything like that ever happened to him.

(Phil) *I never believed any stories about "miracles"; they were kind of like ghost stories to me. I've never seen them and even if I had, I would have explanations for what they were. Something you ate, dreamt, smoked, or drank - just a coincidence. Because of this, I didn't see any value in telling others this story. I just assumed God did it to get my attention and I couldn't explain anything else. When Danny said someone else will tell you to write it, I knew I was in the safe zone – "I haven't even told anyone about it", I thought. I hurried up and agreed just to move on, and said, 'Sure! If God wants us to share this and write it down, He'll send someone else to tell me. I completely forgot that four months prior I had "slipped up" and shared some of the rain story to my co-worker.*

In his tired state of mind, Phil opened up and shared the rain story with Ted. Phil said Ted had never spoken about this again. He said, Ted had showed up in his cube that day at work. Phil said, "Sure - what's up?" "Hey Phil, do you remember a few months back when we were working on that problem together and you told me about the rain story? Well, I was telling my wife about it and I really think you should write that down." Phil was shocked and could only say, "Thanks for the tip; I'll keep it in mind". Phil confessed that he turned around and begin to cry sitting in his cube. That night the kids were writing letters to their grandma in NY who was not doing so good, and I handed the paper to Phil to write a little something to his grandma. He decided to write down the rain story and share what God has been doing in our lives with his grandma.

The next morning, I typed it out what Phil had written. We paid an artist a few bucks to draw a picture for the cover. called it "The Rain" and started to hand it out to share the good news of Jesus with people, and finally it was done - it was a huge weight off my chest. So I figured I would now share it with our immediate friends and family just through Facebook. Well, then I thought how much would I have to hate all my other Facebook friends to not let them know that I had found out God is real? I had accumulated thousands of friends because of all the jobs and the smoke shop and fighting and modeling. So I sat down each morning with a goal to share it with at least twenty to forty people over Facebook.

I remember not feeling embarrassed. I was confident in what I had seen and been part of - and when you know God is real, and you believe Jesus is the answer, it is easy to tell people. I only had two people get mad at me out of thousands. I told them I was sorry what happened to me upset them. They were both anti-God and I remember thinking that if they don't think God exists, why do they get so upset when I say he does? If I told you I saw the Loch Ness Monster and I wanted you to know, you could just laugh and say I was crazy. You would never get mad, but if you get mad when I say I found God, well the only reason is if you actually had doubt it in your heart that God is real - but didn't want to accept it. You are happy with your path and don't want to acknowledge that you could possibly be wrong, because then you might have to change the way you live and think. And, to you, change of mind seems like weakness. You are set in your opinion. Like I said, if an atheist was one hundred percent sure God was not real, anyone proclaiming God is real would never even upset them; they would find it humorous, like a kid who still believes in the Tooth Fairy.

CHAPTER 25: SUICIDE AND FORTY-SEVEN HUNDRED DOLLARS

The Godcidences never stop happening, but they do slow down sometimes. Or maybe I get so busy doing day to day tasks I actually miss some. I still pray every morning and offer the day to God, and tell Him that I will do what He wants before I do what I want. In these chapters, I am sharing some of the coolest things I have been blessed to be a part of.

One night early on in our street team with Scott, we went to the men's shelter downtown, and I remember taking notice of a thirty-five-year-old white man with blonde hair sitting at the cafeteria table as we passed out the food. I later made my way over to him and just sat down by him. He was cute, stocky and looked strong, like a roofer or a construction worker. He was dressed nice and didn't look like he was homeless and in the shelter. But the pain in his eyes with the wounds on his hands and neck was fresh. He had a large white bandage around his whole neck. When he tried to respond to any questions I asked him, his voice would sound awful and raspy. As I hung out with him, I found out he had just got out of the hospital. He was in a street fight the night before and had been stabbed in the neck. We talked for a while but it was very difficult to understand him. He let me know he was wanted, but was just going to go kill himself, rather than turn himself in. He was so sad. He had relapsed and got into this fight and now was looking at going to jail for a while.

With trembling hands and tears in his eyes, he pulled out his wallet. It was a normal man's wallet full of credit cards and pictures. In it was his very attractive all-blonde family, made up of a teenage boy, a teenage girl and a beautiful and tall blonde woman who was obviously his wife. He asked me if I would tell them he was sorry. He wrote down her number and continued to cry and asked me to tell his kids that this wasn't their fault and he was sorry. He had already made up his mind to kill himself. I talked to him and prayed with him. I gave him a stern lecture and hugged him. After about thirty minutes, he promised me he would turn himself in. Much later that evening he called me to let me know he kept his promise and was at the police station to turn himself in.

One night we were all headed to the park to hand out hot dogs and we picked up someone to take to the shelter. The man was a tall, black homeless man who was very intoxicated. He was so drunk he was sitting in the passenger seat making all types of voices, kind of like cartoon characters. Scott was driving and I was behind them, but between the two of them leaning into the front from the middle back seat.

I tried a few times to say something to this guy, but he wasn't having it. He kept shaking his head from side to side while making all these voices and sounds. It was hard to make many words out of all the jabber. Finally, I looked up at the ceiling of the van and in my head said, "God, if you want us to share Christ with this guy you better sober him up or do something." So I looked back at our passenger and said, "Hi, my name is Danny and I'm from Omaha, Nebraska." That guy spun so fast around in his seat and gave me the stinky eye. He said firmly, "I'm Danny from Omaha, Nebraska." So I said, "No, I'm Danny from Omaha, Nebraska." He replied kind of irritated as if I was messing with him, "No," he said, "I am Danny from Omaha, Nebraska." So I figured he was just messing with me and I said, "No, I'm Danny, D.A.N.N.Y, from Omaha, Nebraska." He then said firmly, while glaring around at me, "No, I'm Danny, D>A>N>N>Y, from Omaha, Nebraska."

He pulled out his ID and I pulled out mine. We were both Danny from Omaha, Nebraska! He seemed to sober up immediately, as we chatted about people and places we had been. We shared Christ and prayed with him. I know he didn't leave that van without knowing that God had his hand on his life and was still reaching out to him. It was very cool.

With all these things happening, I remember catching our pastor, Pastor Monica, down at ICCM and I told her about the rain and the guy at the Arts Theater. She said, "You know you are very blessed to see so many things like this. Most people who believe don't get to see that." I went over to sit down after we talked and couldn't stop thinking about what she had said. I was upset with God thinking, "Yeah, God - why don't you just show everybody this stuff and everyone would believe?"

I even felt a little guilty that I had gotten to be a part of so many amazing Godcidences. So I prayed and said, "God, why don't you? Why don't you just come down here and show everybody how real you are?" That's when I heard a soft voice say to me, "But I have." It isn't that God doesn't try to show people; it's that we don't have our eyes open. I was sure God has stepped into everyone's life at some point, but was brushed off as a coincidence and quickly forgotten as if nothing had ever happened. I don't hear an audible voice, I just heard it in my own voice - but that is the third time it has happened.

The first time was with a contractor who had come over our house and all I could hear in my head was, "Tell him about the rain Danny, tell him about the rain." The second time was when Phil and I were in church and just coming out of the shock of the Arts Theater guy approaching me. Phil leaned over during service and whispered, "God has put it on my heart that we are going to be giving some money away to someone." I whispered back, "OK" At this point I'm expecting anything can happen at any time in our lives. Phil leaned back over and said, "God put an amount in my head and I'm having a hard time with it. Would you pray about it and tell me if you get anything?" As soon as he said it, I prayed and a large number, let's say forty-seven hundred dollars, popped into my head. We didn't even have forty-seven hundred dollars!

I leaned over and with a heavy but willing heart said, "It's not forty-seven hundred dollars, is it?" Phil put his eyes into the palms of his hands and I knew it was forty-seven hundred dollars. I thought, "Oh great, well if that's what God wants then so be it." We agreed to keep our ears and eyes open wide for whoever came along with the need for forty-seven hundred dollars. We made a plan to start saving up for something but that person, place or thing never came up. We waited for a year for anything stating forty-seven hundred dollars, but not a single thing. Now I can't help but wonder if God was just seeing if we were really willing and what our hearts reaction would be? Maybe we missed it. But we prayed about it and nothing ever came of it. We give tithe and have more than we could ever need in life. But that's all thanks to God. Because what things I used to think I had to have in my life I see no use for, like the large diamond engagement ring Phil had to work for two months just to buy me. It sits on my shelf and collects dust because I am now too embarrassed to wear it. Thousands of dollars spent on a not-so-precious stone so I could have a symbol on my finger like all the other girls would have. The commercials told me I wanted one and it would prove his love for me. It makes me feel foolish and I wish I could trade it in for something we could all enjoy as a family.

CHAPTER 26: WEDDINGS AND WITNESSING

We hardly ever get to see what God's intentions are or what happens to the people we come into contact with. But one of my favorites is Patrick. Patrick was an independent contractor who was just getting on his feet when I hired him for outdoor maintenance on our home. I liked him like a brother I never had, the second I met him. He was a clown, yet witty and playfully sarcastic. I loved going out to chat with him while he fixed the woodpecker holes in our house and built our dock. He fell in the lake in early spring, filling his waiters up with water, and managed to make even that hilarious.

He had a four-leaf clover tattooed on the side of his neck and was even visually entertaining. His work was solid and he was an honest man. Phil really liked him too. We both see ourselves in Patrick. We would hang out and have jackass conversations with him and it would teeter-totter into real life a little. But we never told Patrick what we did or any God stuff. I think he just thought we were good people who used to be ghetto and moved on up, so now we volunteer to give back. We kept Patrick busy for a while but then he moved on. We stayed in contact with him as friends and contractor referrals.

When he was out at the house working, we got to meet his fiancé. Her name was Victoria and she was a lot like me, so I really enjoyed talking to her. Time passed and approximately a year and a half later we received an invitation from them for their wedding. Phil and I were both excited for them and it had been heavy on our heart because we never told Patrick about our cool God stories. It was just never the right time. We never stopped praying for Patrick and I knew in my heart God, was not finished with him yet. My kids really liked Patrick and were excited for their wedding. When we arrived we prayed in the car for God to use this day for his glory and I knew something special was going to happen. We had not seen the couple for a long time.

They were so cute together and their son was so precious. We had a second to say hi before the wedding kicked off. Standing in a beautifully decorated barn in the middle of an apple orchard, we saw Patrick with some friends. We made our way over and Patrick introduced us to his mother. She was a lovely lady and told me I looked just beautiful. I was flattered because as we get older that kind of complement becomes few and far between. Phil and I walked around as our son looked all over for free food with his sister. Those kids are always on the hunt. I told Phil before we exited the car, "We have three people to talk to and give the rain story to." It seemed weird to me to say it, so I'm sure it was weird for Phil to hear me say it.

We had put our testimony in a card for Patrick and Victoria with a wedding gift. So I felt like we had finally shared Christ with them. We had been praying for Patrick for over a year. He pressed heavy on our hearts and we were not sure why. We would talk about Patrick every so often and knew that he was going to come back around in our lives someday. So when we received a wedding invitation from them we were very excited. After peacefully strolling around the beautiful apple orchard Phil and I walked into the barn all by ourselves and found our assigned seats. We made sure our kids knew where we were and gave them permission to go explore. When Domiano got up and walked out of the barn, I leaned forward to Phil and whispered, "Take one of these flowers and give it to Domiano to wear behind her ear." Phil looked at me as if to say, "OK, sure I will."

I knew he wasn't going to, because Phil isn't the kind of guy to reach into the center piece and take a flower for his daughter at a wedding, not without thinking about how hard someone worked on making that flower bouquet look just right (plus how they probably wouldn't appreciate it if he took one out and messed it up). So with no one in the barn I leaned forward again and whispered, "Just do it. It will be really sweet and cute. My dad did it for me once at a wedding and it's cute. Just do it." I knew how it would make Domiano feel, as she was all dressed up pretty, even if Phil didn't get it, but I was going to make him do it anyway.

Domiano made her way back to us at our table and other guests started to come in and find their assigned seats. Phil sat with his arm around his daughter and he would whisper in her ear and then they would laugh as he squeezed her neck under her ear. I waited patiently for Phil to do what I had told him to do, but he still had not taken a flower out to give to his daughter. So when he made eye contact with me again, I leaned forward and thumped the vase with a flick of my finger - and again Phil gave me a look of, "OK, sure. I will nod my head and pretend that I'm going to, but we both know I'm not going to." At this point I playfully wanted to kick him under the table. I heard an announcement from somewhere behind me and the speaker shouted, "OK, it is time for immediate family to go have pictures taken with the bride and groom."

I heard a chair scrape the floor behind me so I scooted mine in just a bit so they could get by. An arm from that person reached down in front of me and the hand went into the vase in front of me. I followed that hand and looked up to the face and it was Patrick's mom. She reached into the vase and pulled out a rose then gave it to me and smiled. I thanked her and looked over at Phil in complete shock. We both know our conversation about him giving Domiano a flower from that vase took place privately. I shrugged my shoulder and excitedly said, "Well, I guess we know who we are supposed to be sharing Christ with." It was really cool and very crazy. The same crazy thing happened with a man in line and another who walked passed me at the wedding. Phil and I shared our testimony with both men and both were the other two divine appointments.

I stopped one man because I knew it was him, as he was walking into the barn. He was a very good-looking and well-educated young black man, dressed as if he had walked right off the cover of a magazine. I just said "Hi," then joyfully introduced Phil and me. He was from another country and Christ-followers had helped get him to America many years ago. He had a relationship with Christ, but had fallen away with our American ways. He even mentioned it as getting caught up in the ways of wanting more and more or trying to look the best we can and working hard to own the best things that others want but can't obtain. We are constantly looking for entertainment, while pushing things like family aside, in order to be known for being the best athlete or having the best career or to be seen as the perfect family.

I told Him what God wanted me to say to him and it was amazing. I just encouraged him to remember God is first and to talk to him again and every day for everything, like he used to. I knew I was supposed to talk to him and I can't really tell you what that feels like. But I know there was no way I wasn't going to talk to him, I didn't want to know what that feels like. I could just see so clearly who he was, and the words just flew out of my mouth. No, the people I was to talk with that day were not glowing with neon, and no there was no big Jesus arrow pointing down from heaven. It was in the same way you know you forgot something on the way out the door and you remember before you pull out of the driveway. It is intuition on a God-scale and you can't say no. Unfortunately, I'm sure I have rejected that God-intuition more than once on purpose, but God forgives me when I ask for forgiveness. I let it go, stand back up, and start marching back on His path.

Later the music was on, and I was on the dance floor, dancing with my kids. There was a young woman dancing on the floor, and she blurted out that she needed to talk. She was in a bad relationship, and was reaching out to God and felt like she needed to talk to me. I encouraged her to turn back to God, and trust Him. We shared our testimony, and prayed with her, and then chalked it up as another Godcidence. Maybe a lot of people get approached on the dance floors at weddings by people hurting and seeking God, but it was the first time that has happened to us! Later at the wedding, Phil had the opportunity to chat with Patrick's mom when I got up to dance with the kids. He had asked her why she reached in to get the flower and give it to me. She said she had no idea why she did that.

(Phil) *I talked to Patrick's mom; she shared with me how she felt she just needed to get up and give Danny the rose, and she was going to ignore it but came back because she didn't feel she could leave the room without giving her the flower. She shared how she has been praying for years for her sons to come back to Jesus, and felt like she was all alone at times. I reminded her that she didn't even know we existed, but God crossed Patrick and our lives and we had been praying for her son along with her for the past year. Sometimes, we only see the world around us and forget that God is so much bigger and loves us and our loved ones so much more than we can ever imagine. We are never alone because God sends an army to our lost loved one, an army we may never know God had been sending all along.*

This last week, several months after the wedding, God put it on my heart to invite Patrick and Victoria out on Street Team. I used Facebook to invite them. Patrick said, "What is Street Team?" I just told him we go out to feed the homeless and they should come this Friday. They both came out on Street Team and, from what they said after; they both want to go out again. I thought all the praying might be too weird for them, but they were both cool with it. Patrick and Victoria have a wonderful life to live and God is reaching into their lives for many different reasons. I wish I could see what God's going to do. But that's how God works and I'm cool with it.

CHAPTER 27: DIVINE FISHING AND DOLLAR BILLS

One day, we headed out to go fish the Minnesota River bank. We all loaded up and I remember informing the kids that I'd prayed for God to send someone. We headed down Highway 35 until we got off on a side road that, after a mile or two, leads to a spot where a guy was fishing. We didn't fish there, as we were looking for a secluded hidden spot. We parked farther away and walked through some tall weeds and trees and down the river bank a while until we picked the perfect spot.

The current was strong and I hadn't had any bites, when I heard footsteps in the weeds behind me. It was an older white guy. He was dressed nice and not for fishing. I looked at my son Angelo with a, "You know what that is don't ya, look". The guy kept coming straight for me. When he got right next to me I said, "Hi." He said, "I have driven on the interstate past this river every day for three years and wanted to stop, but never have. I always wondered how the fishing is. Any luck?" I said, "We just got here so we can't really tell you; we have never fished here before."

I couldn't help but think of how far he had to drive to get here and walk to ask us that, or why today of all days would he choose to stop and ask. So I asked him, "What do you do for a living?" He said, "I'm a Pastor." Angelo looked and me and playfully rolled his eyes. I knew it and he knew it too. Angelo reeled in his fishing pole and made his way a little farther away as to not be too bugged by the conversation that he knew was about to take place.

I found out that this pastor was just like Phil's childhood pastor who believed God was kind of this all-seeing eye watching over us, not really answering prayers or moving in people's lives. I shared the rain story and the Arts Theater story with him, and then Phil encouraged him for at least an hour to re-evaluate his ideas of what he thinks God is and ask God to lead his life and show him what he has for him. I was grateful Angelo was there to see how odd it was for that guy to just show up like that.

I decided I wanted to get a part-time job when we were living in a temporary rental in Eagan while waiting for our house to close. I prayed about it and asked God to only put me where he could use me for his glory. I opened Craigslist and applied for a waitressing gig at the airport. I was hired on the spot and started the next week. I had really missed talking to people and loved where I worked. People were flying all over the world and I would get to hear them tell me about it.

I get to pray with people who need prayer - mothers going to bury sons, boys and girls going into boot camp, missionaries going off into a foreign land to do God's will, even pastors traveling to spread God's Word. It is amazing that I prayed for God to use me and pick a job out that is best for His will and I get to pray with people at work. I get to encourage the atheists to look up and talk to God and I get to shine the love of Jesus on the lost every day I go to work and that is my mission field for now. I share my testimony with as many as I can and even get to share it with famous people like MC Hammer and Morris Chestnut.

Now after years of working there, everyone knows I'm a Jesus girl. I don't run around screaming it; I usually mention it softly. Some people playfully crack jokes about it and some will even come to me for prayer or advice. One Tuesday, I didn't make any money in tips. Call me spoiled, because I like to try and make a certain amount every day I work. Well, this Tuesday was the worst tip day I had since I worked at the airport.

That next morning, I was on my way to work and I asked God something I had never asked for: "God, would you bless my finances?" I felt guilty even as it rolled off my tongue, because Phil and I are very blessed in finances and it was being a little greedy. That morning I went in and opened the restaurant. My first customer was a kind-hearted older black woman traveling on business, and she ordered pancakes. Unfortunately, our griddle was not hot and her pancakes took twenty-five minutes, which is way too long for any food. She kept a positive attitude about it and I made casual "how's the weather," conversation with her to help pass the time. After she had eaten, she stopped me on my table drive by and handed me a folded-up bill.

All she said was, "God put it on my heart to give this to you today." I said, "Thank you" and went into the kitchen to peek at it. In my hand sat a one-hundred-dollar bill. I was embarrassed and shocked. I ran out to tell her, "You are never going to believe this but I am a believer too and I prayed for the first time ever today for God to bless my finances, even though it is something I had never prayed for and even felt guilty for praying for - and then you gave me this." She said, "God put it on my heart to. Ain't that just how God works?"

I continued to tell her about Street Team and that I would put it to good use. That day every single person who worked in that area of the airport heard about my hundred-dollar bill. My bartender Laura, who was on the fence about God, was able to see what had just happened and I split the money evenly with her - but before that, every person would come up to me and say, "I heard what your God did today!" or "Show me that hundred-dollar-bill!" Then I told the story and said to each and every person that God did not give me a hundred-dollar-bill for me. God gave it to me because He knew I would tell everyone in that arm of the airport about it and the glory would be all His.

But there was even more to it than that, because a young girl who I had not seen for at least three months came walking into the restaurant. She had worked in our gate area, but had transferred to another section of the airport. She knew God, but was on the run from Him. She had come out on Street Team with me once and broke down crying at the altar at church. I was so excited to see her that I marched right over and, with the hundred-dollar-bill in hand, I told her the story. She did not react the way I had expected her to. She looked at me and said, "Danny, I'm pregnant. I have an appointment for an abortion after work."

I stood shocked and was already praying and asking God what to say. I talked to her and told her she must pray about it - and she knew she must pray about it. I laid conviction down on her shoulders for not speaking with her mother about this decision first. She looked up and with tears in her eyes said, "How did you know to say that?" But that's just how God works. I don't know what she chose to do that day. I have not seen her since that day. I do know that Laura my bartender gave her life to Christ and God's will was done that day. Seeds were planted and seeds were watered. Those are the best days of my life.

I was on the way to work before I wrote this book and looked up as I was driving and asked, "God, you're not telling me to write a book, are you?" Because I hate doing things like this and one of my first customers looked up at me after I cracked a joke about his buddy in the bathroom and said, "You're a storyteller you should write a book." I gazed at him for a second and bowed my head in humility.

I shared with him that I prayed to God this morning and asked God if He wanted me to write a book about all the God stuff that has taken place in our lives. I told him God used him to be the second confirmation that the answer is yes. The third was a teacher who said the same thing that night at a Teachers' Conference for my daughter: "You should write a book she said." I bowed my head humbly and right there started to cry. My husband explained to her that I had been praying and asking God if that was what He was telling me to do and we had just talked about it in the car on the way there, and that God had used her to give me a third confirmation. My daughter's teacher smiled and said to me, "Isn't that just how God works?!"

Phil and I have days where we are desperately seeking God's divine appointments; those days our eyes are wide open and we are full of energy for the Lord. We also have an even amount of days where we are not really feeling it, when we would rather lie in bed all day and close the doors to the world and its' needs. But when you commit to pray every morning for God to use you for His glory, it doesn't matter how you are feeling; if God has something for you He knows you can handle it, He is going to deliver what you need to see it through.

CHAPTER 28: LOST BAGS AND BUSTED TRAILERS

Sheri, one of our favorite sisters in Christ from ICCM church, needed help moving one afternoon. She was moving out of the upstairs home apartment into her very own apartment. She had asked us for help and I had agreed. Phil is never too happy when I volunteer us both, especially for moving people. But we both love her so much that it was easy. She was not prepared for moving day, so the house was not fully packed up.

It took many trips with our rickety, homemade open trailer. We had bought it the previous year to carry our kayaks. It was never intended for such heavy and long distance trips. By the end of the first day, Phil and I were not happy campers. It had cost us a couple of hundred dollars in food and gas; plus all her son's stuff, who was in jail at the time, had to go into storage. On the last trip to storage with her son's stuff, we noticed the trailer sitting funny. One corner towards the back end of our Tahoe was sitting down at an angle and low. We pulled over only to find that the welding on the frame underneath had given. It was hanging broken, but it was still drivable. We finished up with unloading the trailer and made our way home.

Phil was tired and frustrated when we got home. You see, we were out doing God's will, not simply doing good deeds. Sheri is a wonderful example of someone coming from a hard childhood and life surrendering to Christ. She is a child of God and He wanted to pour some love on her. We were just doing what we thought God wanted us to do, so why would our trailer break on the first day? We still needed to go back the next day and finish the job. So Phil was sitting in front of the computer and prayed.

(Phil) *"No Good Deed Goes Unpunished" was the words I heard my Dad saying in my head as I looked at the support beam snapped in half under my trailer. My dad was always helping people, and I never saw him turn down an opportunity to help someone, but those words still echoed, and for one second, I listened to the words instead of remembering his actions.*

Then I stopped, stood up, remembered what God had been doing in my life and was filled with confidence that He was going to use this, too. It was after 6 p.m., and I thought there would be little hope of finding someone open, let alone someone to fix this tonight; but I sat in front of my computer, prayed and turned it over to God to use how He needed. I googled 'welding', and figured I'd start calling down the list until someone answered.

I was about to hang up the first call when a guy answers and says, "What?" Not quite the business greeting I was looking for! I asked, "Is this a welding shop? The man said yes, and over the next several hours "What" and "Yes" were the nicest words that came out of his mouth. I was, apparently, an idiot for buying this trailer. I tried to make small talk, offered to help, but everything was met with blasphemy, cursing, and belittlement. I couldn't believe that God was going to work here.

I prayed. "God, if you want to reach out to this guy, you are going to have to open up the door because He doesn't seem to want anything to do with either of us." Just then, he blurted out, "I'm getting too old for this shit", then stopped in his tracks and said, "On the other hand I guess I should hit my knees every day and thank God that I can still work." After hours of getting verbally beat up, I was in shock that "God" came out of his mouth in a non-blasphemous way. I thought, "Oh, is that me? Am I up to bat, God?"

I wasn't sure what to say and asked, "Is that just a figure of speech, or do you believe in God?" That question seemed to infuriate him quite a bit and he started right where he left off only with more intensity and walked away from me while I was trying to follow up my question. I told God that this definitely was not the guy you are trying to reach out to and I'll look somewhere else. After paying the guy, I couldn't wait to get out of there and give my ears a break. I was hooking up my trailer when I noticed him walk up behind me and I thought, "Oh boy, here we go again." He said, "So what are you, real religious or something?"

I couldn't believe this. I've been trying to talk to this guy for hours and verbally getting hit with a bat, and now he wants to know if I'm religious? I stood up faced him and said, "Nope, but I do believe that God is real, His son was Jesus, He died for us and here is how I got to this point." I expected him to shut me down again, punch me, or simply walk away, but he just stood there and stared at me - for one and a half hours.

I shared everything that God had ever done in my life, right up to the point of talking with him, and he never spoke a word. I ended with and that's why I know God is real and I am supposed to be here right now. Then everything was quiet and the rough and tough grown man in front of me started to cry.

He shared with me how his shop closes at 5 p.m., and he only answered my call because it was a 402 area code and his sister lives in Omaha; he thought it was her. His brother had a brain tumor and was having emergency surgery the next day and they didn't believe he will make it; he wondered if I could pray for that. He didn't surrender his life to Jesus that night, and I don't know if his brother lived through the surgery. I just know that God loves each of us and is trying to show just how much, and he can use any opportunity, any person, any time - we just have to say yes, and be willing to take a few blows from time to time.

Traveling is probably my most favorite thing to do with my family. I love that we are trapped together with no distractions and our quality time is at its best. It is an opportunity to give your family one hundred percent of your best attention. Phil's Dad gave him some advice once, saying make sure it's your family that gets your best. Usually, we are sharing our best with co-workers and clients so we are drained when we get home. Phil and I always make an effort to watch that balance. It wouldn't make any sense to give people outside of your family everything you've got, then come home and dump what's left on your spouse and kids. No, you give them your best and everyone else can have what is left.

Well, on the plane to Atlanta to go see Phil's family, I was seated next to a young black man from Africa. He was a doctor and had lots of questions about God. It was an amazing journey of conversation and he was very receiving. We landed and we all walked together with him until it was time to go our separate ways. He was on the fence about God and was sure God had put him next to me for good purpose. We hugged and he even hugged my kids. It was a very special few hours in the air. We went to baggage claim to get all of our luggage, but my daughter's luggage did not show up. We must have waited thirty minutes and still nothing. We still needed to go get a rental car plus drive another three hours to get to Phil's brother Dave's house - plus it was already 9:00 p.m. Phil was trying to keep his cool because all of my specially prepared auto-immune food was in that luggage, and so was all of my daughter's clothes, including the outfit for pictures with the family tomorrow afternoon.

Domiano and I left Phil and Angelo, and headed over to the baggage problem office where an older black woman sat behind a desk in the small room. I looked at her and said, "I am so sorry, I have bad news. One piece of our luggage did not make it to Atlanta with us." She sounded surprised and said, "Why are you sorry?"

I said, "Because that is probably one of your least favorite things to hear from travelers and I'm sure you don't want to have to deal with this right now. You're probably almost out of here for the night. I bet people just lose their marbles over their bags and you probably just dread it when a bag gets lost," I said humbly. She was absolutely blown away. I told her a little about God's grace for me and she got tears in her eyes. Phil and Angelo came into the room and we all started talking about God and how knowing that God is real has changed our lives forever. That woman told us that we were an answer to her prayer. She had had the worst week ever, and just before we came into her office she had been praying telling God she couldn't do this any longer and was ready to just walk out. "But God sent me four angels," she said. We all circled up and prayed, thanking God for giving us all reminders of His love for us and asked for strength for our sister in Christ. I was so full of gratitude for our luggage being lost.

Phil told me that while he kept watching the baggage claim carousel not spit out our bag, he looked up to heaven and said, "God, now I know you wouldn't deliberately let us lose a piece of our luggage unless it was for your purpose. Do you have a divine appointment for us?" It wasn't the first time someone has called us angels, but it was the first time all four of us got to share Christ and be a part of a divine appointment of God's grace together. It was a strong message to our children and I pray they shine the light of Jesus when these situations present themselves when we are no longer around. When things happen to us as followers of Christ, we must look for God's way. Only then will you get to be used by God as a light for others to see Christ in you. Whenever we hand over the bad to God, He makes it beautiful beyond our imagination.

CHAPTER 29: HAIRCUTS AND HEARTACHES

If you have never been up to the Voyageurs National Park or the Boundary Waters, I really recommend it. It is so quiet and peaceful, plus the fishing is fantastic. We booked a cabin in the summer of 2014 inside the Park. Angelo and Domiano were still too young to canoe the Boundary Waters, but Voyagers allows motorized boats in areas.

We prayed about the trip, just like always, telling God we would share Christ or do anything He had for us to do (but please be bold about showing us, or we might miss it). We had a wonderful time just the four of us. We fished and played, and went island hopping to explore everything we could under every rock and tree we found. We love to explore as a family.

This month, I was having a particularly bad hair month. You see, a few months ago I had cut off my beautiful, long, dark brown hair. I had ten to twelve inches cut off to shorter than shoulder length. I was not pursuing modeling or acting anymore and my hair just sat in a ponytail for weeks. Well, now it was slowly growing back and I did not know what to do with it. Honestly, in every picture I took in Voyagers with my family I would look at myself and see my hair and think, "Yuck, I got to do something about this hair." A few days into our trip, it was a cold and cloudy day so we decided to go into a town called International Falls, which sits on the border of the US and Canada.

We were pretty sure with a name like International Falls that it must have a huge waterfall. In the car ride up to the border town, I looked at myself in the car mirror and boy did I look tore up. I decided that as soon as we returned to Lakeville, I was going to set an appointment with the lady who had cut my hair short and get it cut. I decided that I was going to keep my hair short for good. I know this sounds girly, but I was in a girly turmoil over my hair in my own head. I was going back and forth to keep it growing or keep it short. Finally, right before we pulled into town I made a private decision and - no turning back - I would keep my hair short. I never even mentioned my silliness to my family, because they all had opinions on my hair length and their opinion did not matter when it came to how I kept my hair length. They are not the ones who dry it and flat iron it (that takes an hour by the way). So, feeling accomplished with a decision made over my hair, we stopped at a huge border novelty store. It was a giant brick building mixed with Canadian and American novelties. We walked inside the main door and I instantly went to the jam samples because I was starving. Angelo and Domiano were about 5 feet from me looking at kid stuff and Phil was standing next to me. Phil and I were standing at the jams when I could see a woman talking to Angelo and Domiano about the toys. I paid no attention to it because she worked there and I figured she was just getting them excited about a toy so I would get stuck buying it. But in seconds I heard, "Mom, look!"

I hesitantly turned towards my kids and this lady. She was showing them how to use a loon call. Loons are a beautiful duck up north and make distinct calls for their partners and babies. I turned and the lady was handing the loon call off to my daughter. Domiano pulled the string and a disk thing spun fast as she pulled the string apart, making the loon sound. I responded the same way I always do: "Neat, sounds just like it," secretly hoping they would just put it back down and forget about it.

The lady took two steps towards me and as she got right in front of me she rotated around me to pass by me. As she did this, she said into my ear, "I used to have really long hair, but I cut it all off and now I'm growing it out again." She was not making eye contact with me. She said it as if she was telling me a secret. I turned to Phil after she passed by me and said, "Did you hear that?" My brain was locked up trying to process my sanity.

I said again to Phil, "What did she just say to me?" Phil shrugged his shoulders and said, "I couldn't make it out." I spun to the kids, and with my eyes bulging from my skull said, "Hey, did either of you hear what that lady just said?" They both shook their heads and looked at me confused. "Did you hear her say something to me?" Everyone agreed they heard her say something, but no one had any idea what she said. So it finally happened I thought. After all these years, I have lost my bloody mind. I obsessed over my hair so much that, standing in this store full of Canadian brown bears, a worker walked by and said something about bears and all I could hear was something about hair and not bear. I decided I had just been so fixated on my hair looking bad that I just lost my mind.

It would continue to drive me nuts and I would ask each family member again, "Did she say anything about hair or bear?" Nope, no one had a clue. Well, we didn't buy anything and exited the store. Now the store sat on the corner of the street and when Phil pulled out of the parking lot, he took a left then another left and then another, putting us right back on the other side of the building at the back entrance. Phil parked and said, "I'm going inside to pull some fliers." I knew what he meant, and it was to get some of those tourist fliers they always have at hotels and stuff so you can see what there is to do in the surrounding area. Then Angelo says, "I'm going in with Dad!" Then Domiano says, "I'm going in to go pee!"

Now I have to go back in, because Domiano can't go pee alone or in the boy's bathroom so I got back out of the car to go into the other side of the store where we were all just in. I thought to myself, "If I see that lady, I'm going to ask her if she said something about hair and if she says yes, then God I will know it is you." I followed my daughter back into the store, passing my husband and son in the entryway, and when I lifted my head there she was. That lady was walking right to me. There were several people who worked there and she was now right there at the other door walking towards me. When she got in front of me, she turned to the left and stood at the fudge and ice cream counter and just stood there staring as if she was getting ready to order fudge. I looked down at Domiano, pointed out the bathroom to her and told her to go and come right back. I walked over to the lady and stood at her side, kind of staring at her.

I said to her, "Hi again. I have to ask: did you say something about hair to me earlier?" She said, "Yes, I did. I used to have hair so long I could sit on it, but I cut it all off. I have been growing it out, but this is as long as it has gotten so far." As she said this, she grabbed her pony tail and ran her fingers down the length of it. I stood there in shock and disbelief. I was grateful I hadn't started to lose my mind and excited that this was about to be a really cool God thing! She continued to look at the fudge counter almost with a lost in space daydream look. I was standing on her right, just staring at her. I said, "How's your day going?" We made casual weather chit-chat and then she started telling me all the pain she had in her heart. Phil, Angelo, and Domiano all made their way over by us and heard me talking to the lady. They sat down in a small booth in front of the fudge counter for guests.

I introduced her to my family and we continued to talk standing next to the booth, while my family listened. I told them about what she said about her hair, never letting the lady know how amazing it was for her to say such a thing. She continued to tell us about her son who was a meth addict and it was hard for her; and also that today was her grandson's first birthday. It broke her heart that she was not allowed to see him because of, as she put it, "baby momma drama" - the mother of her grandson, because of her own son's behavior, wouldn't allow her to see the little boy on his first birthday.

Then she said, "I was in the car driving to work today, not even wanting to come in. I just feel hopeless and overwhelmed, and all alone. I started praying, and asked God to send someone today to let me know that I'm not alone, and tell me everything is going to be OK." I said, "Well, you don't know this but God put it on my heart to talk to you today. And I was wondering if we could pray with you?" With tears in her eyes she reached her hands forward and we all held hands and prayed. I got her contact information and lost it on the trip. She called us all angels and said we had answered her prayer. Looking out the window on the ride back to our cabin, I remember thinking that it is moments like this that I should never ever forget just how real God is and how much He loves us all.

CHAPTER 30: GOD'S GUN AND GOD'S LAND

The following is one of my favorite vacationing stories to share; it is seriously an amazing, unexplained, chain of events. As soon as we moved to Minnesota, I wanted to go up to Lake Superior. We had heard about it and wanted to see it for ourselves, so in that first summer Phil suggested we just head up there randomly and pitch a tent with Grandma and the kids. While he was sitting in front of his computer, he looked up campgrounds up there. Phil and I are very picky when it comes to where we like to camp. We like to be right on the water and have no one around us as we also enjoy being alone with our family when we are on vacation. So he called the best campsite and asked the lady what they had open for that weekend. She kind of chuckled and informed Phil that he just called the most sought after camping grounds in all Superior and they are booked a year in advance. Phil laughed with the lady and as he was asking her for any other campgrounds he should try, the lady said, "You ain't going to believe this, but just now as we are talking, somebody just canceled our best campsite for this weekend and for the days you just requested. This never happens; you should book right now before it is gone." So Phil did just that.

He couldn't believe that happened and it was kind of strange; so we both know that is how God works - to line things up in our lives to share Christ's message with people. So we got excited to go on this camping trip, even more now because maybe God had something for us to do. We packed up and headed north a few hours to Superior. We had our eyes wide open for God the whole time. We passed a tiny town with a restaurant and a rock shop, and because I collect rocks and fossils I knew we would be returning to the town if we got a rainy day or needed supplies. We pulled into the campsite with the pontoon and all our gear. We checked in and headed deeper into the grounds. We followed a long road until finally we got to a parking lot. The lady at the front desk made a comment about what a great spot we had.

We were excited, but Phil and I don't get our hopes up anymore. We have both been let down way too many times, so we just expect the worse and then get excited if it's anything better than horrible. This mentality works out great because we are never too disappointed. Situated in the corner of the parking lot were large wheelbarrows for your gear. We started to load up and saw it was going to take a few trips. Phil and I each loaded the supplies with a child in the wheelbarrow and headed down with a kid in a barrel, and my mom's dog as well.

We were surprised at how far we had to go with all our gear, but when we arrived at our camp spot we were blown away with the privacy and the view. As we walked down our dirt path we turned into our own dirt wheelbarrow driveway that sat on a pier which overlooked all of Superior. The whole pier was ours alone. We camped thirty feet up and if we climbed down we were on our own private shoreline on Superior. It was magnificent and to our right was a second pier; way to our left was a third. Each one only hosted one family and they were so far away that we couldn't see or hear them. All the campsites we passed, and all those numbers on the map, and we got that spot. We gave God thanks and praise and promised him we would be diligent in sharing Christ. We walked around after pitching our tent and there was a beautiful waterfall and a cove we played at. It was all just stunning. The little chipmunks were stealing all our food and the kids loved it.

We even saw bear claw marks on the bear safe. We pitched the hammock and settled in for a few days of amazing views and quality family time. As we were walking around our huge campsite/pier, I noticed an old slab of cement and what looked like an old broken chimney made of tiny red brick. I was standing with Phil and pointed to the ground on my left and said, "Look, it looks like there was an old cabin here a long time ago. That looks like chimney brick." Phil agreed and we both thought what a wonderful spot to have a cabin.

Just then Phil's phone made a noise and he checked it. "Hey, guess what? That gun I posted on a gun trader website months ago had just sold. It sold for what I asked for it and it even sold here in Minnesota. Looks like we can take it right to a gun shop just 30 minutes south of where we live. Monday, when we get back, we can run it there on lunch; you want to ride with me?" "Sure", I said. "I can't believe it sold; it has been on there for four months and no one has even commented on it." I had forgotten it was even still there. This was good news for us.

We needed the money to help build up for a down payment should we buy a house here in Minnesota. When my Dad passed away we inherited his gun collection. We kept plenty of them, all his favorites, but had to let some go. Well, we played and fished and even prayed with the park rangers we stopped and talked to. I tried to share Christ with everyone we came across, or at least kept my ears and eyes open, and so did Phil. We went into the town and had lunch. I even went into the cute rock shop and bought my daughter a necklace. We took the Pontoon out on Superior and just had a blast. We climbed all over our pier and even found agates on our shoreline. The nights were beautiful and we got to see the full moon rise over Lake Superior. It was one of the most amazing scenes we have ever seen, but we never found our divine appointment or maybe we did and it just wasn't as divine as we thought. God's got it, even if we missed it.

So we packed up on our last day and headed back to Apple Valley. That next Monday, Phil and I headed to the gun shop, south of where we lived, to make the exchange. Phil just went in alone and the guy was not there. The man behind the counter said that this had never happened before and that it was way out of this buyer's character to not show up. One guy called to find out what had happened and the buyer had just messed up the day and was extremely apologetic. So Phil and I headed back home and we were to come again the next day to meet the buyer and do the transaction. We were not upset at all as it was a nice drive for the both of us. So the next day we headed back to the gun store and I decided to go in with Phil this time. I had grown up in gun shows and gun stores with my father. I had shot every caliber of gun by the time I was ten years old.

I went into the gun shop with Phil, just to bring back memories of my dad, but it hurt a little to go. I walked in behind Phil and Phil went over to the counter on the right to talk to the guy he met with yesterday. I walked in and went to the left to the counter to look at all the guns on the wall and in the glass counter display cases. Phil was talking over there, so I decided to make small talk with the guy behind my counter. He was a good old boy. But he knew I was not going to be buying a gun and had no desire at all to have small talk with me. He was very tall and skinny with blonde hair, probably 50-60 years old. He had on a leather biker vest and the wallet chain. You know the type.

Well, I was determined to chit-chat with somebody so I said, "I grew up around guns my whole life, and spent going to gun shows with my dad. He's been gone for a few years, but I still like to look at see what's new." He pointed out a new model he liked and gave me some facts about the weight and maker. I said, "Yeah we are from Omaha, Nebraska and just moved up here a few months ago. We finally made it up this weekend to see your guys' Lake Superior." He said, "Yeah, it's beautiful up there." I said, "It sure is, we got lucky and had the most beautiful campsite in the whole Superior." We were right by this tiny town and it was so fun. The kids had a blast. Our campsite was on a rocky pier that sat between two piers, but ours was the best one. It had an overlook and you could climb down the cliff to the water. It even had a tree perched right at the tip of an arch off of our pier we climbed out to. It was absolutely beautiful."

At this moment, something changed in his tough biker front he puts out for people to see. He had completely changed his body and was slouched. He folded his arms up and tears were forming in his eyes. He said, "Was the town called Silver Bay?" I said, "I don't remember the name." He said, "Did it have a rock shop?" I excitedly said, "Yes!" He said, "Did it have a restaurant that overlooked Lake Superior?" Again I was excited to reply, "Yes!" With tears in his eyes he said, "I know that town, and I know that pier. I grew up there. My father and I built a cabin on that pier together when I was a boy. I spent my entire childhood hunting that land with my dog." He described how he and his father built a cabin that he lived in right on that rocky pier. He described it down to the last boulder, truly outstanding.

I said, "I saw it, I saw where your cabin was, we camped right there." I told him about the cement slab and the broken bricks. He said, "When my father died, we tried to keep the land but the state took it from us and declared the land a state park. They just took it. I told him I was sorry. In my pocket, I had a printed-out rain story and I said. "I think I am supposed to share something with you." I slid it across the counter to him. He picked it up suspiciously, "What is this?" I said it is what happened to me. It is a God story and I think you're supposed to read it. I could see he was deflated and had that 'here we go again' look in his eyes. I said, "Just promise me you're going to read it." He looked at me, folded the rain story and slid it into the pocket in his leather vest and said submissively like a puppy who just got scolded again," I promise you, I will read it." Look at that ... isn't that just crazy, a tough biker guy completely softened by God to hear his word one more time? God goes to great lengths to reach the hardened of hearts. It was insane to me how all that had lined up like dominoes. But that's how God always works. You will be amazed to see just how far He reaches to connect with you.

CHAPTER 31: SPIRITUAL WARFARE AND THE SPIRIT'S TOUCH

All my Godcidences are good, but unfortunately the Devil is real and I came face to face with his puppet one late night on Street Team. Street Team is always safe; we pray a hedge of protection over us and God is with us. His angels protect us as we walk. I am never frightened and ninety-nine percent of people we meet are so grateful and accepting of guidance food or prayer. It is amazing. One night though, out in the parking lot across from Mickey's Liquor Store, the Devil's puppet came crawling. Harsh words, I know, but I was there ... so listen carefully.

We had our two tables set up facing into the corner of the parking lot. One table held the food and drinks with the other covered in anonymously gifted clothes from Community of Hope Church. We had our backs to the cars driving around in the Walgreen's parking lot as people formed a line for food and prayer. A young twenty-something girl came over to the table and I got to speak with her. We chatted, and I honestly don't remember what about, but I noticed she was very innocent-minded. She was too innocent and vulnerable to be out on these streets on a Friday night, especially this corner. Well, I was called away and walked over to a black, fancy four-door car that had pulled up behind us. It was so sleek and it had fantastic dark tinted windows with beautiful chrome rims. I don't know what type of car it was, but it screamed, "Lots of money". I was called and waved to the driver's door, so I went. It was safe; I was right by the rest of the Friday night Street Team crew.

The three in the car were smoking weed and it rolled out into my face. It doesn't bother me, as I grew up with the weed rolling twenty-four by seven in my childhood home. I was even there once, cruising around smoking weed all night and looking for things to do. The driver was the biggest, most good-looking black man I had ever seen. He was so cute and well dressed. If the Vikings had a football player on the loose, I just found him. This angel opens his mouth and with the most flirtatiously sweet voice say, "Whatcha doin out here, baby?" I smirked at him, because he was trying to be cute with me and I'm so past this stage in life. I say to him, "Well, we are a Street Team who comes out on Friday nights to pray for people and invite them to ICCM church down on 18th and ..."

He playfully cuts me off to say, "Wait a minute, wait a minute, it's too cold for you to be out here. Why don't you hop in?" I smirk and shake my head softly and say," My husband and I have been coming down here every Friday to feed the ..." "Shhhhhh," he cuts me off again. "Now which one is your husband?" I nod to a group of people twenty feet away and say, "He's over there, but we come out here to invite you all to chur ..."

He reached out and handed me a card. I looked at the front and started talking as he was still trying to talk over me and say, "You and your husband want a little girl to play with tonight? or maybe a little boy?" As he is still saying this I flip the card and on the back was a woman laying naked on a couch. My heart sinks into my stomach and my head started to feel dizzy from the words he just spoke. He was offering me and my husband a little child to play with sexually for that night. He was a pimp and even had a business card. So I said with a soft voice, "Look, we are out here doing God's will ..." Again, he cut me off and said, "Fuck your God" as he tilted his head back to laugh. I noticed his two clowns were not clowning so much now. I saw the fear in their eyes and they knew they had made their bed this night.

I said, "I have to get back, but have a good night," and I leaned down so I could clearly see his two passengers and said, "May God bless you." I walked away in sadness and in shock. I went over to Scott and gave him the business card and told him something had happened and I was going to just stand in back at the tables for a while. The car continued to cruise the parking lot, like a wolf looking for prey. He was the most charismatic man I had ever met outside my own father. He could easily talk anyone into his car. That night my heart was squeezed and my momentum was slowed with the pain. It is awful the battles they face. Anyone could get talked into that car and probably think nothing of hitting a joint with him. They probably would have been too nervous to turn down a crack pipe or a hit of heroin now that they were fully committed. Do you think he would take them home or sell them to the next guy who called the number on the card?

I believe Scott turned in the card, but where does that get us? Nowhere out there that night. That night I realized it really is a spiritual war. No man would poison his own community and his own people without surrendering over to the Devil's will. Only someone walking in evil can commit such evil acts.

One night out on Street Team I remember a large black man who did not believe in God. I remember talking to him for a while in front of the food table. As we chatted, I was prompted by God to do something I had never seen or even heard of before. God told me in my heart, not my ears, to place my hand on this guy's heart and he would feel God's presence in him. I didn't hesitate a second, I just did it.

I looked at the man and softly said, "Do you want to feel the presence of the Holy Spirit in your heart?" The guy nodded his head in disbelief. I took my hand and placed it directly on his chest where his heart sits. "Do you feel that?" I asked. His eyes were huge and a wave of fear and disbelief moved over him. I saw it. I saw panic in his eyes. I said with a smile and confidence, "That's the Holy Spirit!" I felt nothing in my hand, but I knew he had felt something significant by his reaction. He said, "I can see that's really convincing to people; that's a nice little trick you picked up." I knew he had decided that whatever had happened to him was a crazy trick I can perform. But I thought it was awesome. I only did it one more time and it was with my daughter later that week. Domiano was nine years old at the time and she was lying in her bed. I sat on the floor next to her and we were just mother-daughter chit-chatting. She had already given her life to Christ, but she is so young.

At that time, she may have just joined in because it was what we were all doing. As we talked she asked," Mom, how do you know God is really real?" I told her again all the amazing things we have all been able to be a part of. I was surprised she still had doubt. Part of me thought she was just asking questions to keep me at her bedside longer. But with your own children, just like those around you, the only way to see if they have truly surrendered their lives to Christ is by their actions. So God prompted me again to place my hand on her heart so she would feel the Holy Spirit. I said, "Domiano, do you want to feel the Holy Spirit in your heart?" She nodded her little head. I took my right hand and placed it over her heart and touched it. Domiano instantly reacted in a loud cry and tears. Her knees moved up to her chest as she balled up, weeping.

In shock I asked, "Did you feel Him? Did you feel the Holy Spirit?" Through serious tears and out-loud wailing she nodded her head. I held her in my arms and thanked God for giving her such proof. I felt relieved knowing she knows the truth and the decision is hers to make. This was the second and last time I was ever prompted by the Lord to act so bravely. It was awesome and I still can't believe it, even as I type it out.

CHAPTER 32: ELEPHANTS AND ETERNITY

Back in Omaha I enjoyed making extra cash on the side whenever I could. I would model for print and commercials for extra cash, plus I liked to buy antiques at garage sales and sell them on eBay for profit. Chandeliers, guitars, saxophones, whatever I found that I could turn a profit on, I would buy and sell. About thirty days before we moved to Minnesota, I went to a sale that had a huge collection of three hundred elephants called The Herd and I paid the guy three hundred dollars for the whole set. It was an amazing deal because on eBay they were selling anywhere separately for five to two hundred dollars each. I was going to pick up a lot of money off of these elephants.

Each elephant came with a box, so in went three hundred small medium and large boxes, just stuffed in my car, and because we were moving I would have to wait until we moved up to Minnesota to post them for sale individually on eBay. It was no fun moving them up here to our rental house. We knew we were probably going to rent again before we found our permanent home and there was no way I was going to move all those elephants from house to house to house. So I decided to post all of them on Craigslist for three hundred dollars to just get rid of them. I did not have the time to sell them individually anymore.

I got an email about the elephants a few times on the condition and price from a girl named Nicole. Finally, she showed up one day to buy them. It was her, her boyfriend and a man she called Dad. Nicole, my mom and I laughed the whole time with a giggly girly conversation. Somehow, they had to make all those boxes fit into the back of a compact car. My mom and I must have talked to Nicole for about twenty minutes. I had mentioned to her that I was giving the three hundred dollars to a single mom I had met through my daughter's music lessons. This mother's daughter was in the hospital and I wanted her to have extra Christmas money. The truth is I told her my true intentions with the money to make sure she didn't try to barter with the price. We laughed some more then she paid and left.

Months later, life looks so much different for me, God has wrecked my world at the Arts Theater, I'm all in with Jesus, and now people probably look at me the way I looked at them, like a "big old Bible thumper". One day me and my mom had gone for a walk and got into a huge argument. We were still arguing when we walked into the door of our home. During the argument, I grabbed a flower vase and pounded it on the kitchen counter and it exploded. A piece of glass flew at my mother's face and she was furious. She accused me of being just like my grossly abusive father and stomped out of the house.

I was horrified; I was, beyond words, disappointed in myself. I had been my mom's protector from my father my whole life and I just behaved like my crazy dad. She forgave me that day, but later that night I could not forgive myself. I was up late praying and crying in bed, sobbing like a child while telling God how sorry I was and begging Him to still use me to share His word with others. I was so devastated. I remember asking, "God, how can you use me to share the message of Christ with the broken-hearted out on the streets every Friday when I'm failing in my own house with my own mother?" I asked God, "How can you trust me to tell strangers who don't know you about your message of salvation when I just lost my mind on my mom?" That is when my phone made a beep beep beep sound.

I wiped the tears from my eyes; they were so swollen I could hardly read the text. It said; "Danny, this is Nicole ... the girl who bought your elephants. Call me". It was late at night. Everyone else was sleeping and I looked up and said, "God, is this you?" I thought there was no way God wants me for anything, let alone to use me to talk to some lady I sold elephants to six months ago on Craigslist. But I jumped up and called her. Nicole was hysterical and she was crying. This is what she said to me: "Danny, do you remember me?" "Yes", I said. "Danny," she yelled into the phone, "I don't know what to do. Why is God doing this to me? I remember you were kinda funny and I am laying here asking God why He is doing this to me and your name keeps popping up in my head." She continued to cry out that her boyfriend had gone downstairs and killed himself with a gun. When he did, his brain matter went all over the boxes of elephants and they came in and took him - and now she has to bury him.

Also, her son was in the house when it happened. She told me her son's biological father was now going to try to take custody by saying the son was living in an unfit home. She had been with her boyfriend for many years; however, everything was in his name. His parents blamed her and drained the bank account and were kicking her out of the home. She said, "Danny, I remember you seemed like a good person, but I don't know what to do." I had no idea what to say except, "Nicole, I think I am supposed to pray with you", and I did. We prayed, although I don't remember what was prayed.

The next day I went over to the town home they lived in, where I helped move stuff up from downstairs where he had killed himself. She did not want to go into these rooms, because it was too difficult for her. I shared the message of Christ with her mom and grandma, her son and a few other people while I was there, telling them that God is real, that God is with them and loves them; that God sent His only Son to die on the cross for all our sins, and when we believe this and confess it to God with our mouth we turn from our sin and give our lives to Christ. According to the Bible, God's Word preserved for all generations, this belief and confession is our only passage into heaven. Not by good deeds, not by giving money or going to church, not by joining a religion - just by accepting God's gift. John 3:16.

Her boyfriend was buried and I did not hear from Nicole until a few months later when she called again. In tears, she asked me why God was punishing her. I told her, "He is with you now and always has been." She asked, "Why is God killing me, because I was just diagnosed with brain cancer. Why is this happening to me?" she cried. I prayed with her again telling her to give her life to Christ and ask for God's guidance and peace. A short time later, Nicole died from cancer. I realized God's forgiveness for us is swift. He needs us all to do His will before our own. Look at how far out from Nicole God had to reach to find someone to share Christ with her, to encourage her to reach to God because He is there - some random lady she bought elephants from on Craigslist. I pray Nicole gave her life to Christ. I gave her my testimony in a pamphlet named "The Rain". In it is this prayer of salvation. In my heart, I believe she gave her life to Christ.

These coincidental meetings with strangers go on and on in my life, because God is in love with each of us, and He wants us all to go to heaven when we die. Love God, love people. These are His words. Jesus said all the law and the prophets could be hung from these two: love God, and love people. That is our part; He will take care of the rest. We all fall short of God's glory, every pastor, street minister, man, woman and child. We are full of vanity and pride and lust. If God only used perfect people to reach people and do His will, he would never use any of us. The key is just to say yes, not next year, or tomorrow, or even later today, but right now just tell God "Yes". It doesn't matter what imperfections you have, God sees His Son when He looks at you, and wants the very best for you. There is no greater peace and purpose that will give you satisfaction then to submit your life to God.

These are a few of the true events, of so many that I am ashamed to say I have become numb and used to the joy when they happen in my life. Can you imagine being so used to miracles that you are spoiled to them? It's a shame. I wish I could show you, but I can't. I wish I was a writer and would write them all down for you to read, but I'm not. I can promise you the Creator of the universe is with you and waiting for you to stop talking to yourself and to talk to Him. God wants you to go to heaven, but you have the freewill to choose. I can share all my God events with you, but ultimately you have to choose to give your life to Christ.

When Nicole came and bought the elephants, she didn't know she was going to be taking her last breath in less than a year. When her world seemed to be crashing in around her, her boyfriend taking his own life, the custody battle, and losing her home, she still didn't know her life would soon be ending. She asked God if He existed and, if so, why was this happening to her. He found someone to bring the answer. Winston Churchill said, "Men occasionally stumble over the truth, but most of them pick themselves up and hurry off as if nothing ever happened." What will you do? Will you ask? And when the answer comes, will you respond? Or will you just dust yourself off?

CHAPTER 33: JESUS AND THE JOURNEY

So now that Phil and I have committed to be all in for Jesus, I have become one of those people that I was sure had lost their minds. I'm confident in my faith that God is real and Jesus died on the cross for my sins. We have officially jumped with both feet into the living water. God put it on our hearts to join Scott Stover's Street Team. Phil and I are slow to respond to God's way. We are stubborn and still take baby steps. We want to make sure if we are doing something it is because God wants us to. So we need signs of confirmation from God that this is what He wants us to do.

I don't want to just do good deeds, but I really only want to do 'God deeds' now. Only if it serves God's purpose for my life; we don't want anything other than God's Will to take time away from our family. We continued to attend ICCM and soon we learned about their discipleship program. We decided to pray and committed to take two days away from our kids to attend if it was something He wanted for us. Neither one of us wanted to do it. We are lazy and love spending time together. We really don't like to take time away from family time. But I was encouraging a prostituted girl to join the ICCM Discipleship class that would run for one full year every Thursday night and every Saturday afternoon. Phil on the other hand was hanging out with a pot dealer who was a struggling alcoholic with a fiancé and six kids. Phil had met him one night out on Street team. The kids were inside the house while dad would sit on the porch and sell pot and drink with his buddies. Now this was an all-black neighborhood and here came Scott, Rick, and Phil - white guys from the suburbs to share Jesus.

Phil became good friends with the dealer and we even got to regularly pick them all up for church. Getting the dad into discipleship would be a huge step. One day, the dealer told Phil he would do the discipleship program if Phil did it with him. The same day, the prostitute told me she would do the discipleship program if I did it with her. That very morning, Phil prayed and asked God that if He wanted us to take the discipleship class, we needed to have those two sign up as well.

We immediately signed up knowing it was what God wanted us to. The funny thing is both partners signed up the same day that Phil prayed asking God, and neither one of them ever showed up for a single class. Phil and I continued to go to the class, and it was great; we had fun in the class being the only white people and it was fun for everyone else too. Several times in my childhood, I was the only white one and it never bugged me a bit; and the same thing with Phil - we were both comfortable and felt no discrimination or even different. I don't think we ever saw black or white growing up, we just saw people. Same goes with my own children's viewpoint, to them, people are just people, all of us, God's children.

Black or white is just descriptive of a picture painted when you're talking color of skin, not a category to place people for us. Sometimes we dreaded going to class, but once we got there we enjoyed ourselves. Some of our classmates were still in their mess of crack or weed. It was hard for some to talk, while others couldn't stop. We were like the class that was held after school for detention - it was a lot of fun. I learned so much about God and the things I was learning were coming true in my life right before my very eyes. Now remember I was never born and raised on the Bible. I was a proud atheist up until twenty-two years old. So I remember very clearly when we covered the 'turn your other cheek' bit of the Bible in our discipleship class at ICCM.

It was an open discussion and Slim was speaking. Slim was in the class with his girlfriend Shyia. Slim got very agitated at the thought of walking down the street, and a thug walking up to him, punking him out, making him look weak. Because if he looked weak he would become a target in the hood and this 'turn your other cheek thing' ain't going to work in real life. He was upset that Pastor Monica was not going to see His way and couldn't see that God's way don't work out there. He said if he did that, he would be shot in the back walking down the street.

A lady in our class was going to be moving that week and asked us for help. We agreed to move her stuff out of storage and into an upstairs apartment in a shared home. Well, she was older and had bad knees so it was all up to Phil and me to move all her stuff. It was awful and we vowed to never move anyone again, unless God tells us again of course. This was the fourth time that year moving, and we were feeling spent. It turned out that God had other plans, but this time the drive was long and it took two days with several trips. She was excited to be moving out of a shelter, but you know it hardened my heart to just have her stand and watch the whole time! To add insult to injury, the apartment was up a winding staircase with stairs so tiny they would never make code today. On the first day, we were about half done unloading the truck when a short, stocky thirty-year-old man came rushing out at us from the downstairs apartment.

He yelled, "Who and the fuck do you people think you are? I'm trying to sleep down here and you're making all this fucking noise." I thought about discipleship class and the turn your other cheek bit. Normally I would have been so mean and vulgar to this man. He would have walked away, because I always made sure my bark was the biggest. I had the meanest, most personally vulgar, tongue that you can imagine. I learned from a master manipulator how to verbally slice grown men in half. But today, I'm "Danny the Bible thumper" and I'm in discipleship class being taught God's way. "I am so sorry," I said with sad, humble eyes. "We are moving her into the upstairs apartment today and I promise we will be quieter."

Now inside I wanted to knock him out a little. I wanted to tell him off. But I was humble with God's way. "Well, I fucking hope so because you ruined my fucking day." He stomped off down the sidewalk. In my mind I thought we had started moving into the apartment at 10:00 am that day, not 6:00 am, and he was leaving anyway. But I did it God's way. I still wanted to do it my own way, because my way is more fun - especially with an audience of anyone. We moved her, and Phil and I rolled our eyes about the guy and just moved on. The next afternoon we were back moving the rest of her stuff into her apartment when the guy came out. "Hey, I just want to tell you I'm sorry about the way I behaved yesterday," he said. "I didn't mean to come off like that." He introduced himself to us and we all shook hands. That week in class I shared what had happened when I did it God's way and how it really worked. Then the lady we moved told us, "You know that guy carries my groceries up all the stairs for me now." All I could think of was how amazing it was. God's promises are true. I get to see it every day now.

My daughter had gotten bullied by someone two grades higher than her on the bus over what seats were what. I sent her back the next morning to apologize to the girl and tell her she didn't realize it was her favorite seat and tell her she promised to never sit in it again, and to hand her a sucker. That mean girl has apologized twice to Domiano about the way she had behaved over the seat. God's way has yet to fail me in my experiences. I am constantly learning to trust in God's way more and more on this Jesus Journey.

I'm humbled by God's will in my life all the time. But when a day or week or even more goes by without something absolutely amazing happening, I find myself wondering if I'm still on the right path. I stay diligent praying and listening to sermons and sooner than later "boom", God uses me again for His purpose in my life. It is the coolest part of my day when it happens and I share it with anybody who will listen.

Think about it for a second, exactly how did this book come into your hands? This is not chance, God is reaching out to you as well!

That first winter going out on Street Team with Scott and Rick was some of the most wonderful Friday nights I had ever had in my life. Looking back at the "Before Jesus Danny'" I am amazed at how I thought being almost famous and being cool with the cool people was good fun, but walking with God and surrendering to His will is so much more.

ICCM church was going to host an indoor bingo night for the families in the shelter. It is absolutely freezing outside here in February, so we sent vans to pick up families and bring them to church for bingo. I remember Pastor Denise, who is the children's pastor, told me I would be in charge of keeping the little ones together and she had a Veggie Tales cartoon for them to sit down and to watch. I thought she must be crazy, because kids are not my thing. Yes, we have two kids of our own but OPK's as I liked to call them ("Other People's Kids") were not at all where my heart was. But I am firm and kids will listen to me, plus I would never tell a pastor no - so I agreed to the challenge.

As the kids came running in, I noticed how wild they were. Ages two to ten and there were about twenty-five of them, running and pushing kicking and biting, I had no idea what to do. I just stood in awe at the chaos happening right at my feet. Pastor Denise said firmly, "I need you to keep the kids in this section of the room." So with orders from her I grabbed a kid running past me and again told him, "You need to do what I said and sit down now." I had grabbed his arm and held it firmly. That little six-year-old looked at me, squinted his eyes at me with hate and started wiggling his arm to break free as if a crocodile had a hold of him - all the while giving me a dirty, "I will kill you" look."

I was in shock because that was the best I had for my drill sergeant style of parenting. He took off running and I looked over at Pastor Denise like a deer in the headlights. She turned and said; "One" and I saw the little crazy rug rats running around and she said, "Two" than they started running in a closer circle by the TV. They knew they were supposed to be sitting in front of. By the time she said, "Three", they had all found a spot and were seated almost quietly. It was like a magic trick. She did not know half of these kids. I was meaner and tougher than her. This made no sense to me and I was sure I would never be working with kids after that, and absolutely positive OPK's were never going to be where God would be using me or my husband.

So now we are part of the children's ministry at ICCM and have been for the last couple of years; it is funny how that works out. Phil and I are exactly where we never knew we always belonged. Our children are a huge part of the ICCM children's ministry as well. We get to work together serving with Pastor Denise nearly every weekend, and God continues to teach us so much.

We have seen amazing turnarounds from the roughest of kids. Moving from cities, like Chicago, or St Louis where their aunty, brothers, fathers, and even grandma have been murdered. They come running from violence, abuse, gangs, prostitution and drug addiction. These are the ones who come guided by God's hand into ICCM Church. My family and I have the privilege to show love to all their children. We whisper kindness, love and Jesus into their little ears.

Just last week my Domiano was invited to a kids' Wednesday church night at a wonderful church doing great things out in the suburbs by our home. She went and found two new ideas for us to try at ICCM for our kids. When she got into the car she told her father, "Dad, I have two new ideas we should do at ICCM. One is to play this game called 'two truths and a lie' and the other is called 'stump the teacher.'" Phil looked shocked and turned to see her face and asked, "Did you talk to your mother?" "No," Domiano replied. Phil had woken up the night before and then woke me up to tell me of two ideas he had about kid's church. Yep, you guessed it! Phil never has new ideas so it was weird for him to bug me with one while I was sleeping. Domiano was so excited that she had been used as confirmation to Phil by God to move forward with something.

She later wrote it down as her first ever Godcidence. So you can bet we were excited that Sunday for kid's church to see why God wanted us to incorporate this into service. We played and the kids enjoyed the prizes and the stump the teacher challenge. We prayed out and dismissed all the kids after class. Phil went to the door to hand out candy and say goodbye to the class. As the kids were leaving, one little girl stayed behind and stood there looking up at Phil. We will call her "Dee". "Dee", being small for a nine- year-old had reached up and tugged on Phil's arm. Phil looked down and bent over to her and said, "Yes, Dee?" "Mr. Phil," she said softly, "I have a question for you for stump the teacher." Phil was delighted and couldn't wait for another dinosaur or angel question.

"Go ahead," he told her, she said, "Mr. Phil, if God is really real, then why did he let my stepdad rape me?" Phil's heart sank into his stomach and he said, "Let's sit down to answer this question." Phil motioned to me to come over and I did. I saw something real was said and we answered her as a team. I told Dee that God doesn't hurt us; God does not do things to us to punish us. I let her know that God was right there begging her stepdad to stop, pleading with him not to do what he was doing and that what he was doing is wrong. God spoke into his heart telling him to please stop what you are doing and turn from your evil ways. But your stepdad did not choose God's way. But God also was there and is still with you. He loves you and is hurt that you were hurt. He wants to use you to help other little girls who have suffered like this. Because you will understand how they feel and will know what to say to them to comfort them. I told her to pray for her stepdad's soul because he does not know God. I understood now why she was so reserved all this time. Now in kid's church she is starting to come out of her shell and shine.

CHAPTER 34: BIGFOOT AND BABIES

I pray every time before I even think about touching the keys on this keyboard. I pray for God to bind up my own tongue of its stupidity and ignorance and pride and that I wouldn't be writing this to you unless it is for God's purpose and not my own. I never wanted to write a book of my testimony, I just wanted to tell everyone what has happened and has been happening to me and my family. Seriously, how much would I have to hate every person I know to not tell them that I know God is real and this is why? That is not something you keep to yourself because you are worried people will think you are strange. Maybe they will, but I have to tell you and everyone I meet that God is really real and if you just reach up in prayer to Him He will reach back. He promised you He would. Why wouldn't you want to?

God continues to put people in our path or us in their paths. At the grocery store, FedEx store, restaurants, street corners, Facebook, emails, phone calls, contractors, and Craigslist, everywhere we look someone is there. He is constantly trying to reach out to each of us. We realized that it is usually a two-way street, if we are listening. He is trying to speak to all of us, and wants us to be a part of this.

Do you think you need to change things in your life to have God love you? God loves you in your mess! The Bible tells us that Jesus died for us while we were still sinners. Do you think you need to be a better person or live like the Bible tells you to before you can even start talking to God? God says that whoever calls on the name of the Lord will be saved. I was a mess and still fail daily, but God is with me and knows I could never be perfect. I am a basket case of daily mistakes. I still snap at people and have hate trying to well up in my heart. I still want to punch people in the face from time to time, but have gotten much better at not doing so. I catch myself bad mouthing someone or pointing out their worst weaknesses. I give it to God every day in prayer and start off strong, but I stumble and fall every single day then ask God to forgive me in prayer later when I reflect over my day.

When I had failed with my mother, God still needed someone to reach Nicole; my failures didn't change that fact, and I had failed miserably. I poked at her with a stick, deliberately making her feel crazy and stupid. When I prayed that night and asked God to please forgive me, and I prayed with tears pouring out my eyes and down my face telling God how awful I am and crying "Please God; please still use me for your purpose!" at that very second the phone rang and it was Nicole. She was calling, she said, because my name kept popping up in her head at that same moment.

God forgave me the second I asked and used me for His glory immediately after, because God needs us all. Yes, even me, even you, in our busy mess we have accumulated. There is nothing cooler than walking with God. Don't judge it unless you are in it. Walking and talking with God and knowing He has things for you to do are the most amazing experiences you will ever be a part of while you are alive in this world. You will never be able to be a disciple of Christ like this again and if you are not in with both feet you are missing out on the greatest thing you will ever be able to accomplish in your life on planet earth. You get to be part of the one and only God experience that comes with giving your life to Christ in prayer and surrendering to His will in your life.

I can only attempt to explain how supernatural it is. You have just got to see it for yourself to believe it. I pray and ask God every day to use me for His glory. I pray before I walk into the store for God to use me for anything that would be His will. I pray and ask God to let me shine the light and love of Jesus on anyone He wants me to. Some days I am selfish and I don't pray and usually nothing exciting happens that day, but I get in bad moods and want to be left alone. I attempt to keep it in check and make sure it does not trickle outside onto others, but sometimes I still fall short and am not perfect.

None of us are perfect, not a single one of us are. It must break God's heart to see anyone who loves Him and has surrendered their lives to Christ pour out false judgment onto others for not being perfect. I have seen signs, which read things such as, "God hates gays." Do you seriously think God hates anyone He created? No, He loves us all equally just as we should love like Christ does and love all our brothers and sisters equally. Our focus as God's disciples should be to point everyone to Christ. Because God will speak to their hearts about what He wants from them. We just have to encourage everyone to open the door to Jesus and let Him in.

We need to show them how peaceful it is to be living water for all to see. I have a hard heart for people who judge other people. I know I'm judging them as well and it is wrong as well. Being a follower of Christ and judging others for what sins they do that are different from what sins you do, does nobody any good. It only makes me not want to follow you for judging me. Judging others is not something you can hide. It is visibly seen by all those around you. If you want to stop judging other people, you must pray for a transformation of your heart because faking it will not work. Those who are judged feel it pierce their heart by your eyes and they will want to turn to their sin faster. You definitely don't want to be anybody's reason for running away from Christ.

If you don't believe that God exist, look at it this way; if I told you I saw Bigfoot the other day you would laugh at me. If I told you I back packed hours into the woods to sit on a giant boulder where the sun shines through the clouds at 2:00 p.m. in a clearing where Bigfoot will show up, you would still call me crazy. If I told you it was in a spot where cell phone and recorders won't work because of reasons I don't understand. You would still say I am nuts. I'm not trying to convince you that these stories are real, that God is real or that Jesus is really re-al. I just want you to go to the boulder and look for yourself, with your own eyes, then make your decision. How can you tell me there is no God, when you refuse to come out and sit on the boulder with me and see for yourself?

I wish I could have a camera on my shoulder all day every day to show you the wonderful Godcidences I get to be a part of. I can't prove to you that God is real with my testimony, but I can get you over to the boulder in the wilderness to look and see for yourself. That's all I'm asking is for you who are reading this and do not believe or are on the fence or have fallen away or are even mad at God. Just give your life to Jesus with all your heart; don't just say it to say it, pray diligently from your heart. If you want to see God, if you want answers God will show up and you will live with a peace that surpasses all earthly understanding. If you are walking with Christ, I hope this encourages you to keep steady on your path. Ask God every day for guidance, read your devotions, get your butt to church and teach your children God's way. Be the shining light for all those who sit in the dark. Shine so bright with kindness and love, that it blots out the darkness and it will transform you into a leading disciple of Jesus Christ. Just like Nicole, you don't know when you will take your last breath, so make every breath count.

God bless you for taking the time out of your life to read my life story and my journey with God. I pray peace be with you and that if God had a message for you He will point it to you immediately. I pray over you and your life to never stop seeking truth and to know God loves you more than you could ever imagine, even in your mess. He loves you.

Danny

Update:

Before I submit this to my editor, I want to tell you what I found out the other day at work. A young lady I regularly work with showed up for her shift and said, "Guess who I saw today working in the airport?" "Who?", I asked. She told me she had seen an old friend. I recognized the name, it was the girl who I ran into the day I received the $100 bill, the girl who told me she had an appointment for an abortion that day after work. So I asked, "How is she?" My friend answered, "She's fine." I looked at her with a need-to-know-more glare and said, "No, how is she doing?" My friend replied, "Well, she is doing good but it's gotta be hard being a single mom of twins."

Made in the USA
Columbia, SC
12 February 2020